T0360701

# Talent Management in Small and Medium Enterprises

*Talent Management in Small and Medium Enterprises* contributes to the body of knowledge concerning talent management in small and medium enterprises.

Despite the growing number of publications on talent management in recent years, research has focused mainly on large companies. As a consequence of this research bias towards large companies, the presented theoretical concepts and practices have limited applicability for talent management in small and medium enterprises (SMEs). Because SMEs constitute a significant part of the national economy in a large number of countries, many authors report the necessity to investigate talent management in such enterprises. This book will be a source of useful data for managers of SMEs and owners and provide them with information about the practices and methods concerning the acquisition, development and retention of talented employees who may contribute to the success of SMEs and the execution of business strategies.

The book offers academic researchers, postgraduate students and reflective practitioners a state-of-the-art overview of talent management in small and medium enterprises.

**Aleksy Pocztowski** is professor and Head of Human Capital Management Department at the Cracow University of Economics, Poland. Aleksy served as a Dean and Vice-rector for research.

**Urban Pauli** is associate professor at the Human Capital Management Department at Cracow University of Economics, Poland.

**Alicja Miś** is associate professor at the Human Capital Management Department at the Cracow University of Economics, Poland.

# Routledge Focus on Issues in Global Talent Management
*Series Editor: Ibraiz Tarique, Pace University, USA*

**Talent Management in Small and Medium Enterprises**
Context, Practices and Outcomes
*Aleksy Pocztowski, Urban Pauli and Alicja Miś*

For more information about this series, please visit: https://www. routledge.com/Routledge-Focus-on-Issues-in-Global-Talent-Management/book-series/RFIGTM

# Talent Management in Small and Medium Enterprises

Context, Practices and Outcomes

**Aleksy Pocztowski, Urban Pauli and Alicja Miś**

NEW YORK AND LONDON

First published 2021
by Routledge
52 Vanderbilt Avenue, New York, NY 10017

and by Routledge
2 Park Square, Milton Park, Abingdon, Oxon OX14 4RN

*Routledge is an imprint of the Taylor & Francis Group, an informa business*

*Library of Congress Cataloging-in-Publication Data*
Names: Pocztowski, Aleksy, author. | Pauli, Urban, 1979– author. | Miś, Alicja, author.
Title: Talent management in small and medium enterprises: context, practices and outcomes / Aleksy Pocztowski, Urban Pauli, Alicja Miś.
Description: New York: Routledge, 2020. |
Series: Routledge focus on issues in global talent management |
Includes bibliographical references and index.
Identifiers: LCCN 2020017836 | ISBN 9780367468538 (hardback) | ISBN 9781003036340 (ebook)
Subjects: LCSH: Small business—Management. |
Personnel management.
Classification: LCC HD62.7 .P63 2020 | DDC 658.3—dc23
LC record available at https://lccn.loc.gov/2020017836

ISBN: 978-0-367-46853-8 (hbk)
ISBN: 978-1-003-03634-0 (ebk)

Typeset in Times New Roman
by codeMantra

This book came into being as a part of project no. 2016/21/B/HS4/01593, "Talent Management in Small and Medium Enterprises," financed by the Polish National Science Center.

# Contents

# Figures

# Tables

# Boxes

# Foreword

*Talent Management in Small and Medium Enterprises: Context, Practices and Outcomes* is an important and timely instalment in an exemplary Routledge collection of volumes on talent management. What makes this book especially valuable is its focus on managing talent in small and medium-sized enterprises (SMEs), which is still an under-researched area that deserves more attention from scholars and practitioners alike. The authors designed their research study in the attempt to address essential issues that have not received due consideration in the extant literature on the subject. These issues revolve around the questions of how SMEs understand the concept of talent, how they define as a talented employee, how both internal and external contexts shape talent management practices in SMEs, how talent management practices in SMEs differ from those employed by large organisations and how these practices influence the effectiveness and growth of SMEs. Both scholars and practitioners can find something valuable in this book. Academics, for example, will appreciate a comprehensive literature review on the subject at hand as well as the new theoretical model of talent management in SMEs developed by the authors using the example of Polish organizations, while practising managers will certainly welcome some implications of this research as well as the data provided as a result of the study.

I hope that you will find an opportunity to read and use *Talent Management in Small and Medium Enterprises: Context, Practices and Outcomes* in your professional work.

Prof. Vlad Vaiman, PhD
School of Management
California Lutheran University, USA

# 1 Introduction

Talent management arose as a field of interest for researchers and managers in the early 1990s when academics and practitioners realised that there was an increasing gap between the levels of supply and the demand of people who can considerably contribute to the performance of firms. Recent analyses have emphasised that seven out of ten corporate leaders spend more than 20% of their time on talent management activities and that talent management has become a critical item in the decision-making processes (Scullion & Collings, 2011), and one of the challenges faced by contemporary enterprises (Van Ark, Mitchel & Ray, 2016). A growing interest in talent management among researchers and practitioners has been reflected in a large number of publications in scientific journals (Dries, 2013; McDonnell, Collings, Mellahi & Schuler, 2017; Nogalski & Tyburcy, 2019).

Despite the fact that talent management issues have been investigated for three decades, research has focused mainly on large companies. In the English language literature (Boudreau & Ramstad, 2005; Scullion, Collings & Caligiuri, 2010; Tarique & Schuler, 2010; Vaiman & Holden, 2011; Festing, Schaefer & Scullion, 2013; Skuza, Scullion & McDonnell, 2013; Collings, 2014; Sparrow & Makram, 2015; Festing, Harsch, Schaefer & Scullion, 2017) as well as in Polish publications (Borkowska, 2005; Listwan, 2005; Pocztowski (Ed.), 2008; Pocztowski & Buchelt, 2009; Ingram, 2011; Kopeć, 2012; Tabor, 2013; Leczykiewicz, 2014; Przytuła, 2014; Tyburcy, 2015; Skuza, 2018), authors have presented theoretical approaches, the findings of empirical research, and descriptions of practices and outcomes of talent management; however, these mainly refer to large companies.

As a consequence of this research bias towards large companies, concepts and orientations in defining talent and talent management mainly refer to practices applied in large companies, often multinationals, and they have limited applicability for talent management in other organisations including small and medium enterprises (SMEs), which comprise a considerable share of the national economy of many countries and in the global economy alike (Krishnan & Scullion, 2017). Approaches referring to management in general, including talent management used in these enterprises, are by no means smaller versions of similar systems employed in large organisations. They stem from the specific context of the functioning of SMEs (Pocztowski, Miś & Pauli, 2019). In light of the above facts, it may be assumed that there is a cognitive gap in talent management in SMEs. Due to the fact that SMEs constitute a significant part of the national economy in a large number of countries, many authors report the necessity to investigate talent management in SMEs (Festing et al., 2013; Valverde, Scullion & Ryan, 2013; Sparrow, Scullion & Tarique, 2014; Krishan & Scullion, 2016).

In the European Charter of Small Enterprises approved by the European Union (EU) leaders in 2000, it is stated that:

> small enterprises are the backbone of the European economy. They are a key source of jobs and a breeding ground for business ideas. Europe's efforts to usher in the new economy will succeed only if small business is brought to the top of the agenda.
>
> (European Commission, 2000, p. 7)

On the basis of statistical data, it can be stated that the total number of companies in the EU-28 was about 27 million in 2016 (Eurostat, 2020) and that micro, small and medium-sized enterprises accounted for the overwhelming majority of enterprises in the EU (99.8%), and provided the majority of employment (66.6%) (European Commission, 2017).

SMEs benefit from the use of knowledge, skills, attitudes and the abilities of their employees, but they should also take measures to increase the value of existing human capital through development programmes or by creating conditions in which new knowledge can emerge. Moreover, due to their characteristics (mobility, flexibility, adaptability, decision-making process, closer relationships with customers), SMEs are an important source of innovation. These innovations refer to introducing new or improving existing goods or services, business processes, marketing or working methods (Oslo Manual, 2005).

Bearing in mind the diversified approach to human resource management in SMEs, it should also be assumed that talent management practices may be executed differently there than in large companies (Pauli, 2018). Despite the fact that the scope of such practices may be convergent with practices in large organisations, the way they are implemented and executed may be different. It ought to be emphasised at this point that SMEs themselves are not a homogeneous group. Regarding the number of employees, which greatly affects the architecture of the human resource management system and talent management alike, micro, small, and medium-sized enterprises can be distinguished. There may be several reasons for the diverse approach to talent management in SMEs. First, such organisations function in a specific business environment (connected with a particular market, location), and the context of their functioning may determine the implementation of unique talent management practices (Krishnan & Scullion, 2017; Gallardo-Gallardo, Thunnissen & Scullion, 2019). Cultural conditions in a given country are one such factor (Skuza et al., 2013; Valverde et al., 2013; Festing et al., 2017). Second, talent management policies and practices are closely connected with a company's growth stage (Krishnan & Scullion, 2017). Young enterprises in their survival or take-off stage will implement different solutions than companies in the prime and maturity stage. Third, the shape of talent management in SMEs depends on the owners' awareness of human capital as a competitive factor and their familiarity with human resource management methods, including those regarding talents (Pocztowski & Pauli, 2013). The owners or managers often lack proper education, and the number of employees and the adopted business model do not justify the employment of human resource (HR) specialists.

The issue addressed by the authors of this book concerns analysing the shape and scope of activities aimed at managing talents in SMEs and identifying the possible impact of such practices on firms' performance. The main goal of the study was to identify and map practices of talent management in SMEs and to look for common patterns. As highlighted in the literature, SMEs may undertake different activities aimed at maximising the use of human capital. These activities are dependent upon the characteristics of SMEs, the context in which they operate and the resources they have. Moreover, in contrast to their larger counterparts, SMEs very often do not have HR departments (or even positions) responsible for executing HR tasks, especially those which are comprehensive enough to be involved in activities such as talent management. This means that in many SMEs, talent management may not be run systematically and the scope of activities undertaken significantly differs from the solutions implemented in large companies. Thus, the main questions we asked while designing our research were as follows:

1   How do SMEs understand the concept of talent and who is defined as a talented employee?
2   How do the internal and external contexts shape talent management practices in SMEs?
3   Do SMEs introduce talent management practices, how can they be characterised and how do they differ from those in large companies?
4   How do talent management policies and practices impact upon the effectiveness and growth of SMEs?

On the basis of the authors' analyses of literature covering talent management and SME management, it can be concluded that these issues have not been investigated in previous research. Moreover, there are no complex studies aimed at presenting the characteristics of talent management in Polish SMEs. A lack of consideration regarding SMEs' specificity while analysing talent management seems to be a cognitive gap covering the issue of talent management as well as human resource management. With this book, the authors would like to contribute to the increase of knowledge concerning talent management in SMEs and also address the above-mentioned gap.

On the basis of the literature review, a theoretical model of talent management in SMEs was developed by the authors. To examine this model, quantitative research on the subsequent stage was conducted. This served to gather sufficient data to create a cohesive description of talent management practices in Polish SMEs. A sample of 200 randomly selected SMEs has provided a distinct overview of the topic. The questionnaire was addressed to CEOs and/or HR managers of Polish SMEs. The interviews were conducted between July and August 2017. Size limits for the inclusion of SMEs in the survey had to comply with the definition of SMEs provided by the EU; however, in order to capture human resource management processes, companies employing fewer than 20 people were excluded. This exclusion was applied on the basis that in such companies, internal schemes and procedures may not be incorporated.

The first stage of the quantitative research relied on the verification of selected SMEs with use of the Computer-Assisted Telephone Interview (CATI) technique. This was aimed at checking whether the companies had introduced any practices addressing talents or high potentials and resulted in creating a proper database, including companies to be interviewed personally (CAPI technique) in the second stage. Such an approach makes it possible to evaluate which practices covering talent management have been introduced in SMEs, whether they are influenced by the external and internal contexts and whether there is a relationship between talent management practices and business, organisational and HR-related outcomes. Furthermore, 18 qualitative in-depth interviews were conducted between November and December 2018 aiming at gaining an insight into the subject matter of talent management in SMEs.

The structure of this book reflects the research approach applied by the authors. In order, the four main chapters cover theoretical issues of talent management including a model of talent management in SMEs; characteristics of contextual factors determining talent management practices; the analysis of talent management practices in the examined SMEs; and a discussion of the business, organisational and HR-related outcomes in different clusters of SMEs practising talent management.

The authors hope that the theoretical dissertations presented in this book, and especially the talent management model comprising internal and external contexts, as well as the interrelations with SMEs' outcomes and empirical findings enabling the identification and clustering of talent management practices, will enrich the existing knowledge in the field. On the basis of the abundant extant global literature in the field of talent management, the authors have attempted to present the specificity of talent management in SMEs from the perspective of Poland as an emerging market in which SMEs play a significant role and talent management issues arouse increasing interest from both researchers and managers.

# 2 Talent Management in a Changing Environment

## The Notion and Dimensions of Talent

Since the end of the 1990s, talent-related issues have been present in literature and addressed in both empirical and an increasing number of theoretical studies. It is a subject of research and theoretical deliberation aimed at identifying the essence of talent, on the one hand, and recognising nuances related to the meanings depending on specific contexts and perspective, on the other. The fact that the two approaches – narrow and broad – coexist increases ambiguity and a lack of coherence, which in effect, inhibits finding a consensus when defining talent.

Reaching a consensus, or at least coming close to it, could help determine the frames of company activities regarding talent management. The significance of talent management tends to increase when the ever-more competitive environment is taken into account. The key arguments behind this are organisational needs connected with human capital, which greatly influence a company's future market position (Vaiman, Scullion & Collings, 2012; Björkman, Ehrnrooth, Mäkëla, Smale & Sumelius, 2013). Dries (2013) identifies two categories of demographic risk faced by modern organisations. The first (resource risk) concerns the decreasing quantity of expert human capital resulting from the fact that the generation of baby boomers is currently reaching their retirement age. This entails losing accumulated expert knowledge and experience for companies. Due to its size, the incoming generations unfortunately do not make up for the loss. The second kind of risk (productivity risk) concerns the increasing level of costs connected with retaining older employees in the company. Calo (2008) lists costs connected with their work (outdated qualifications, decreased motivation, etc.) as examples. Organisations seeking new sources of competitive advantage has focussed on the employees who make considerable contributions towards reaching strategic goals, and at the same time, are not imitable. However, the identification of such individuals is difficult, which amplifies problems with their retention and development.

Solutions aimed at identifying talents are diverse. They partly result from the internal context of the given organisation and partly from the managers' knowledge. 'Talent' is a term that has the potential to give rise to ambiguity. Whilst there is a relatively intuitive application of this term, there are likely to be subtle yet significant differences between how individuals interpret it. Thus, the practical effect is diverse and impossible to compare.

The starting point for considering the substance of talent is identifying the cognitive perspective, which will enable a coherent explanation of the term. Historically, talent was first perceived as a measure and then an individual predisposition. Later it was referred to as a 'natural ability' that should be nurtured and not wasted. This ethical context persists and is present in dictionary explanations. The authors of these explanations advocate the understanding of talent as 'a natural ability to outperform in a given field without special training, a kind of giftedness'. They emphasise that talent is an innate quality rather than a product of personal choice (Thunnissen & Van Arensbergen, 2015). Organisational practice shows other approaches to talent; thus, the adopted cognitive perspective is a key context to define the term (Bolander, Werr & Asplund, 2017).

When giving talented individuals theoretical consideration, it is worth referring to the psychology of creativity and to the works of Amabile in particular. According to this author, talent is connected with creativity and it comprises three major components:

- expertise and related skills as the foundation for all creative work in a given field;
- creative thinking, which includes being open to new ideas, self-discipline, an ability to concentrate effort for long periods of time, tolerance for ambiguity, orientation towards risk-taking and a relative lack of concern for social approval;
- intrinsic task motivation driven by a deep interest and involvement in the work, by curiosity, enjoyment or a personal sense of challenge (Amabile, 1997; Strelau, 2015).

The psychological perspective in explaining talent comes down to several dimensions seen in the organisational interpretation of talent (Huselid & Becker, 2011). Talent is perceived as giftedness – possessing and making use of one's natural abilities in a particular domain, which qualifies the individual to be in a group of the best 10% of people of a similar age. The main criterion is perfection in one specific domain (Simonton, 1999; Gagné, 2004).[1] Similarly, from the perspective of psychology (the psychology of work and organisations), talent means the crystallisation of self-concept in the environment of a particular profession and identifying with it. The criterion here is the possession of a clear and stable perception of long-term aims, interests and talents (Oettingen, Marquardt & Gollwitzer, 2012). However, from the perspective of positive psychology, talent is a personal and psychological strength, with an individual's characteristics allowing them to perform well or at their personal best. It is connected with self-actualisation, which means that an individual can make use of and engage their full potential to achieve everything they can (Wood, Linley, Maltby, Kashdan & Hurling, 2011).

From the point of view of human resource management (HRM), talent is understood as human capital (a competence resource, knowledge, social and personal attributes, applied, for example, to generate economic value), social capital (the sum of possessed and obtainable resources that may be mobilised because an organisation's members belong to a social network), political capital (recognition as the criterion of choice) and cultural capital (sustained habits and traditions transmitted from generation to generation and becoming part of the organisational memory) (Farndale, Scullion & Sparrow, 2010). It is closely related to the resource-based view and the main criterion of value is the talented individual's contribution to the organisation's success. The resource-based view encourages considering employees' competences from the perspective of their contribution to the organisation's key competences, which increase the organisation's competitiveness. Thus, emphasis is placed on building human capital by means of internal processes if, as a result, key competences are strengthened. The contribution may be measured by its value and uniqueness, which differentiates organisational solutions in talent management. From the perspective of capital, emphasis is placed on internal processes of developing workers in an organisation when the effects are relatively useful for future outcomes. Regarding transactional costs, emphasis is placed upon individual performance and its monitoring. It requires well-developed processes of precisely diagnosing competences and of adjusting them to appropriate job positions (Lepak & Snell, 1999; Jamka, 2011).

The above-mentioned perspectives and approaches to talent-related issues stress its interdisciplinary character, but at the same time, they show conceptual boundaries of the subject with its varied definitions and multiple contexts.

Professional literature offers an abundance of talent definitions. Comparing these makes it possible to select specific features of talent identified by various theoreticians and researchers. It enables the creation of a map of different meanings of talent, which makes the subject more comprehensive and its understanding more homogeneous. The academic perception of talent places it in the field of scientific disciplines, adopting the perspective which is dominant for a particular author (Ulrich, 2011). However, organisational explanations followed by proper practices focus mainly on an organisation's needs and its specificity, which strongly affects the way in which talent is approached and talent management is executed (Tansley et al., 2007). Comparing and contrasting the two points of view is promising. This makes it possible to identify common areas in the approaches as well as those which may be completed by or enriched with features not previously taken into account.

Defining talent may refer to features of an individual or a group:

> the superior mastery of systematically developed abilities or skills.
>
> (Gagné, 2000)

It may focus on a specific contribution of individuals to an organisation:

> talent means the total of all the experience, knowledge, skills and behaviours that a person has and brings to work.
>
> (Cheese, Thomas & Craig, 2008)

Sometimes talent is defined as a whole group of employees:

> is essentially a euphemism for 'people'.
>
> (Lewis & Heckman, 2006)

It is also defined by means of uniqueness:

> a pool of employees who are exceptional in their skills and abilities.
>
> (Silzer & Dowell, 2010)

Some authors emphasise the role of performance/outcome:

> those workers who ensure the competitiveness and future of a company.
>
> (Bethke-Langenegger, Mahler & Staffelbach, 2011)

Other authors also refer to defining talent from the perspective of a given organisational strategy and goals:

> those individuals who can make a difference to organizational performance, either through their immediate contribution or in the longer-term by demonstrating the highest levels of potential.
>
> (Tansley et al., 2007)

From the development perspective, there is the question of whether talent is constant or is influenced and shaped by an organisation.

> A set of competences that, being developed and applied, allow the person to perform a certain role in an excellent way.
> (Gonzalez-Cruz, Martinez-Fuentes & Pardo-del-Val, 2009)

The above-mentioned definitions are merely a part of the existing denotation of talent and they show the most common terms associated with it. In the majority of cases, talent refers to the abilities and skills of an individual, often their competences, potential, thought patterns and behaviours. Sometimes, correlations between talent and knowledge, development, input, outcomes, as well as individual performance occur. In some cases, talent is associated with a group, a team or its part.

The connotations of talent resulting from practice are also worth considering as solutions proposed by organisations are usually unique and they take into account the current needs of the given company. In many cases, the designation of talent applied by organisations is situational (Pocztowski (Ed.), 2016). Talent is very often understood as an individual attaining high performance. A talented employee performs well in a particular environment, so their talent results from situation-based requirements concerning attaining tasks. They possess the right level of skills and experience with reference to a given job position. Another indicator of talent in organisational practice is expertise and professionalism. Talented employees have extensive knowledge and experience within their competence. Here, the criteria of talent are strictly profiled and precisely defined competences, which take much time to develop and which are rather rare in the labour market. Another designation is above-average knowledge, so innovative people who seek new knowledge, who can experiment with new skills and information and who achieve unique results are considered to be talented individuals (Miś & Pocztowski, 2016). Talent perceived in this way is distinguished by an employee's above-average eagerness to learn and their extensive knowledge going far beyond what is needed in an organisation, which results in the high employability of such talents.

It may be assumed that from an organisational perspective, talent is associated with performance, abilities, skills, potential and knowledge. The difference between theoreticians' and practitioners' operationalisation of talent becomes evident and it is revealed in the level of details in observations and the minor common area of understanding talent by both groups. What supports further discussion concerning the term 'talent' is its practical applicability. It should be emphasised that in the basic approach (the psychology of creativity), talent means a strong curiosity and a drive to deepen it further (passion) as well as an intellectual disposition (associated with intelligence). Such an understanding of talent does not appear in either theoreticians' or practitioners' explanation of the term.

The above theoretical and empirical interpretation may constitute a basis to classify different ways talent is understood depending on the dominant approach to defining the concept. Each dimension is a continuum rather than a separate area (Thunnissen & Van Arensbergen, 2015). The first dimension is the subjective versus objective perception of talent. The objective approach means that a talent is an individual with their extraordinary characteristics (abilities, knowledge, competences). The subjective approach refers to people as a group (as one entity); thus, an organisation has talented personnel or a talented team (Bratton, Garavan, D'Annunzio-Green & Grant, 2017). Another division focuses on inclusiveness versus exclusiveness. The inclusive approach means treating all employees of an organisation as talents. It is assumed that all workers have strengths, which in appropriate circumstances can become valuable for an organisation (Devins & Gold, 2014). The exclusive approach defines talents as an elite set of employees selected from among all employees. It is a group of workers having specific desirable features. It is based on the segmentation of the internal labour market and the identification of selected outperformers and high achievers.

Although both perspectives are most frequently addressed in publications, they limit the perception of talent. They simplify it and focus only on a fragment of reality. Therefore, certain attempts to put them together have been made, such as the models proposed by Gallardo-Gallardo, Dries and Gonzalez-Cruz (2013) and Iles (2012).

The first model places the inclusive/exclusive approach within the objective/subjective perspective. The second model presents two dimensions describing talent: exclusive/inclusive and individual related/position related.

All in all, it is critical to decide whether talent is a gift or an acquired property (Stahl et al., 2012; Thunnissen & Van Arensbergen, 2015). This differentiation is at the very heart of the subject; many researchers from the domain of the psychology of creativity advocate the theory that talent is a gift. Others consider it as a natural ability resulting from an individual's intelligence, creativity and eagerness to go beyond the limits imposed by rules and stereotypes (Hinrichs, 1966; Meyers, van Woerkom & Dries, 2013). In this approach, talent is difficult to manage, teach and train. Talented individuals have unique personalities that are hard to mould in an organisation. Mastery is a variation of acquired talent which stems from an individual's practices and experiences constituting a cumulated value in the form of high performance exceeding the norms and common expectations. Very often, it is associated with competences, particularly in HRM.[2] Talent perceived in this way may be moulded in an organisation and mastery in key areas of the organisation's functioning may be attained. The outcome matters the most, so talent evaluation is based on the individual's input in the organisation. Another approach perceives talent as fit. It refers to the fit between an individual's specific talent and the operating context in which it is used (organisational position). It makes talent more relative than absolute and subjective rather than objective. Context-based perception of talent also emphasises performance and outcome and it does not have a universal character (Coulson-Thomas, 2012).

In the subjective approach, talent may be either inclusive or exclusive. The first type, as previously mentioned, means treating all or large groups of employees in an organisation as talents. Many authors stress the significance of people in creating an organisation's value, which makes it the main determinant of organisational performance (Crain, 2009; Nijs, Gallardo-Gallardo, Dries & Sels, 2014).[3] The exclusive approach assumes that only selected employees may be classified as talents. Thus, talents are the individuals with the highest level of potential demonstrated by their immediate contribution to task performance, leading to observable differences in organisational effectiveness (Tansley et al., 2007; CIPD, 2015). Different indicators of talent may be distinguished here. The first is based on above-average performance in a given domain (Bratton et al., 2017). High performers have a greater input in the organisation, they are more innovative and do their job with more passion. They mould their organisation's competitiveness by attaining above-average performance levels. Another indicator of talent placed within the exclusive approach is high potential, where potential refers to the ability to progress and develop by means of available growth and development processes. In the organisational context, this means that an individual has special properties (motivation, capabilities, skills, abilities and experience) to perform well and undertake other roles contributing to the organisation in the future (Silzer & Church, 2009). Other authors add the category of time (*do it faster/in a shorter time than others*) (Peppermans, Vloeberghs & Perkisas, 2003). Martin and Schmidt (2009) argue that recognising an employee as a high potential is usually based on previous ratings of their performance (halo effect), which may be an inadequate determinant and thus prevent talent management success.

Conceptual frames of talent also embrace talent as input into an organisation (motivation, ambition, interests) and the outcome of their performance. Another approach emphasises talent's universalism – context-independence versus context-dependence (Dries, 2013; Gallardo-Gallardo et al. 2013; Meyers et al., 2013). The above-mentioned dimensions are not contradictory; they constitute a range in which talent means differentiated intensity of particular dimensions and their configurations (Thunnissen & Van Arensbergen, 2015).

In each organisation, talented employees are a specific group for which unique practices and solutions are created within talent management. What differs in an organisation's perception of talents is their value and the universalism of their properties. The fewer the individuals that qualify to the group of talents, the greater is their value for the organisation. A talent is placed and described on the continua of inclusive–exclusive and subjective–objective, with an emphasis upon input (Lepak & Snell, 2002). The second dimension – universalism - refers to context-dependent (situational, non-transferable) versus context-independent (transferable) talent (Bollander et al., 2017). A talent in this approach is placed and described with the use of two dimensions: (1) situational (non-transferable, context-based) – transferable (context-independent) and (2) preordained – learnt, with an emphasis on output. Organisational operationalisations of talent may be precisely indicated by using these two dimensions as the basis for classification (see Figure 2.1).

The first quadrant (VL–UL) considers talent to be inclusive, so all employees are included in a talent pool providing that everyone has some important elements in their potential. Talent is believed

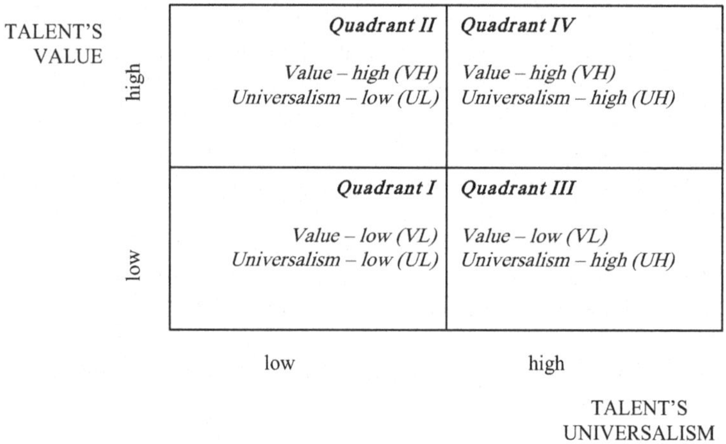

*Figure 2.1* Dimensions of talent.

to be learnt, so it may be modified and shaped/developed in compliance with the organisation's needs. Individual contribution/input is a measure of talent here.

In the second quadrant (VH–UL), talent is exclusive, learnt/acquired as well as being situational, with an emphasis on output; it refers to people who have in their potential some elements that somehow distinguish them from other employees (they achieve above-average performance, stand out due to their expertise, specialised professionalism in certain organisational aspects). Talents are anchored/bound to the organisational situation and stem from it.

The third quadrant (VL–UH) concerns the approach that may be classified as being inclusive. Talent is learnt and transferable and the organisation puts an emphasis on the outcome of talented employees' performance (output). This approach treats all, or at least the majority of employees, as talents. However, as the market value of the employees' talents is high, there is a risk of losing them.

The fourth quadrant (VH–UH) corresponds to the exclusive approach, according to which talent is inborn (giftedness) and is thus independent of the situation (universalism). As it is immediately recognised by the organisation, the focus is on input. The talent instantaneously becomes a value for the organisation. Talent is totally independent of the context/situation (remuneration, position) and does not become outdated.

Bollander et al. (2017) propose a different organisational indicator of talent. Based on their research, the authors indicate four connotations of the notion reflected in the configuration of talent management practices. The indicators are described by means of the previously discussed criteria of talent. They have formulated the following types: *humanistic, competitive, elitist* and *entrepreneurial*.

In the humanistic type, all employees are seen as talents (subjective and inclusive approach), who have developed throughout their lives. They bring certain characteristics to the organisation contributing to the organisation's success (both input and output are important). Talent is situational (context is essential), which means there is a chance to retain it longer in the organisation (it is not universal).

In the competitive type, a talented employee is perceived as a unique configuration of personal characteristics (subjective approach). Thus, there is a limited number of such individuals in the organisation (exclusive approach). Their excellent performance and high potential set them apart and entail future achievements (output is essential). They bring their talent to the organisation (endowment) and it has a high market value (universal-transferable); it becomes the subject of competitiveness.

In the elitist type, talent is extremely unique and rare (exclusive approach). Talented employees exhibit a set of inborn features (giftedness). Their above-average properties make their performance unattainable by others (both input and output). Talent is universal (transferable), so there is a strong desire to retain them in the organisation.

In the entrepreneurial type, all employees are potential talents if they find the right environment (inclusive approach). The emphasis is put on what an employee brings to the organisation (input) and on the features that may be significant for an organisation (subjective); the performance results from motivation, energy and responsibility. A talent is closely linked to the organisation and its culture (context-dependent) and stems from it.

The typology proposed by Bollander et al. (2017) constitutes another attempt to explain and define the term 'talent'. In this sense, it is a step forward both in the cognitive and practical meaning as it applies more diversified criteria of describing talent and its multiple configurations. Although it casts some doubt (e.g. inseparability of the indicators), it enables making more adequate decisions in the field of managing this unique resource.

The above criteria of talent, their configurations and interpretation in management pose a dilemma in formulating an acceptable definition of talent. Taking into account the theoretical and practical context, it seems reasonable to adopt a 'hybrid' approach, including both these criteria. *Talent means inborn abilities of an individual developed throughout their life, which in a specific area (areas) lead to excellent/remarkable performance exceeding norms and expectations set in a company.*

Talent seen from the perspective of an organisation is inborn, it reveals itself in the configuration of individual features of an employee (personality and skills), it develops as a result of individual and/or organisation's intentional activities of the and it is measured by performance (perceived as individual perfection or an excellent performance compared to others). A specific area may refer to individual interests that are comparable with a passion or a function- or post-related performance (e.g. leadership, expertise). It may be characterised as exclusive and more context-based than universal.

Professional literature in management raises the issue of determinants influencing how talents are perceived in organisations. One of the key aspects is an organisation's size. Krishnan and Scullion (2017) argue that defining talent in large organisations cannot be imitated in small enterprises and it needs to be fitted to their specific conditions. This stems from structural conditions: SMEs' internal structure requires employees to have more universal competences; in such companies, organisational structure as well as job positions and related tasks are less precisely defined; managerial competences are usually less professional. Moreover, a growing organisation has more difficulty identifying pivotal positions that need specific skills and competences. They are usually unable to develop them adequately. It should be mentioned at this point that personnel functioning in small and medium enterprises is rather informal (also unprofessional) (Dundon & Wilkinson, 2009), although this does not diminish their competitiveness (due to their greater flexibility). A lower lever of formalisation and a more individualised management style result in a less restrictive selection of candidates and it thus limits the formal identification of talents (Valverde et al., 2013). This is why small enterprises tend to perceive talents in an inclusive rather than exclusive way (high potentials occupying strategic posts). On the basis of the situation and organisational needs, it seems reasonable to emphasise the significance of the range of competences rather than their level of detail and context reliance. Performance is evidently stressed here (output) instead of extraordinary potential, the effects of which may be substantially deferred. Defining talent whilst taking into account the specificity of SMEs sector will *be inclusive, learnt rather than inborn, situational (non-transferable) and focussed on output.*

Summing up the presented considerations, it may be assumed that solving the dilemma of talent's indicators will make it possible to precisely indicate the 'object' of management, which will facilitate designing the right solutions in talent management structure and practice. This trend is already observed in the existent literature in the field.

## Theoretical Approaches to Talent Management

As mentioned in the previous section, talent-related issues have become the subject of intense interest for both researchers and practitioners dealing with management over the last 20 years since a report heralding the war for talent by McKinsey group consultants was published (Chambers, Fouldon, Handfield-Jones, Hankon & Michaels, 1998). The 'war' was predicted to result from companies' growing concern for providing a sufficient talent pool – the prime source of competitive advantage of organisations in the 21st century in the conditions of a knowledge-based economy, technological innovations, globalisation and demographic changes. Many publications on talent management consider the release of the report to be the beginning of an enduring and growing trend encompassing academic research, consultation programmes and practical applications within talent management. It has been reflected in the magnitude of papers on the subject, published in high-impact international journals concerning management, and particularly HRM since 2008 (McDonnell et al., 2017). The trend has also been observed in Polish professional literature in the form of thematic publications, academic papers and talent management programmes implemented in organisations operating in Poland (Pocztowski, 2018).

The growing number of academic research and talent management practices applied in organisations have shaped different approaches to talent management, its goals and range including processes connected with talent acquisition, development and retention. The choice of a particular perspective in defining and approaching talent is a vital factor determining talent management policies and practices, which has already been discussed in the previous section of this chapter. In the mainstream literature concerning talent and talent management, four recently developed perspectives or approaches to talent management may be distinguished (Collings, McDonnell & McMackin, 2017). They are based on a combination of two dimensions of perceiving talent in an organisation: inclusiveness versus exclusiveness and people versus positions (Iles, Chuai & Preece, 2010).

In the first perspective defined by *'people–inclusiveness'* dimensions, talent management assumes that every employee has a certain talent that may and should be developed. Thus, talent management programmes should be addressed to all employees. It is clear that in this perspective, talent management may serve as a new name for HRM and be its rebranding. Such opinions are still to be encountered in some practical publications, but in most cases, the differences between the two concepts are presented (Iles et al., 2010). It may be assumed that currently, there are three main depictions of the relationships between talent management and HRM. The first treats talent management as a new name for HRM. The second considers talent management to be an integral component of HRM. According to the third approach, the assumptions and mindsets that underlie talent management are different from those behind HRM. The above perspective entails huge expenditure on programmes aimed at talent identification, development and retention, as well as the risk of losing talented individuals due to their universalism and greater transferability into the labour market.

This perspective should also include the question of talent management in the context of human resource development (HRD). The HRD concept is closely related to talent management, especially in the field of developing talent. Assuming that the concept of human resource development concerns individual and collective learning, including the context of improving performance, talent development constitutes an interesting basis for analysing both theoretical hypotheses and practical applications that are characteristic of talent development (TD) and human resource development (HRD) and, in a broader perspective, talent management (TM) and human resource management (HRM). There is a gap in professional literature in this respect as the relationships between talent management and HRM (Iles et al., 2010) and between talent development and human resource development are usually approached separately (Stewart, 2017).

In the second perspective, talent management is determined by the *'people–exclusiveness'* dimension where talent is defined as an employees' special skills and abilities to attain high performance at work. HR activities in acquiring, developing, motivating and retaining talents are selectively addressed to groups of high potentials or high performers (McDonnell et al., 2017). The exclusive or elitist approach to talent management does not assume that talent is determined by a position or an organisational role. It is rather based on employment segmentation and a desire to build a segment of talented employees making up the core of employment and to whom special work and remuneration conditions are addressed. Such an approach entails certain risk connected with the right selection of talents for talent management programmes and it may lead to the disappointment of those who have not qualified for the programmes. When applying this approach in talent management, it should be remembered that we deal with individuals who have inborn and rare above-average qualities that are of high value for both an organisation and the labour market.

In the third perspective, talent management is determined by *'position-inclusiveness'* dimensions, where positions are not ranked as all job positions are significant and they all contribute to improving performance and building a competitive advantage. This approach supports internal cooperation in organisations limiting the negative effects of hierarchical structures referring to the mentality and behaviours of organisation members. It is expected to build social capital. In practice, it requires greater expenditure on investments in human capital and dealing with particular matters and interests of different groups of employees or other people working for an organisation. From the perspective of talent management, it is assumed that the value of talents for an organisation is low, the same as their universalism on the labour market, which results from their commonplace availability and context-dependence.

In the fourth perspective, talent management is determined by *'position-exclusiveness'* dimensions. It emphasises the need to attract talented individuals referred to as *'A players'* to an organisation for pivotal positions referred to as *'A positions'* (Huselid, Beatty & Becker, 2005). According to this approach to talent management, it is crucial to determine key positions in an organisation first and then to identify talents so as to fill the positions in order to provide high performance *(A positions–A players–A performance)* (Iles et al., 2010; McDonnell et al., 2017). Such an approach exhibits exclusiveness traits addressing talent management activities to a narrow group of outperformers occupying pivotal posts and justifying it by means of the requirements of the rational allocation of limited financial sources of the organisation. This results in employment segmentation and its division into three main categories:

the above-mentioned outperformers of type A occupying pivotal positions; reliable workers attaining high performance occupying supportive positions make category B; the remaining positions and workers make category C, which does not create significant value for an organisation and may be considered for outsourcing. According to this approach to talent management, when making decisions that concern development and the retention of talents, their value for an organisation as well as their lower universalism on the labour market is taken into account.

Despite some simplifications resulting from the adopted criteria of division, the above approaches to talent management illustrate the ways talent management indicators are defined in professional literature. They are apparently related to the above-mentioned perspectives of defining talent. Depending on the applied definition of talent, the question of inclusiveness or exclusiveness in the approach to talent management arises, hence addressing HR practices to all employees or just selectively to a group of individuals regarded as talents. The inclusive approach makes talent management and development closer to HRM and development. In turn, the exclusive approach distinguishes talent management by identifying key organisational positions and roles as well as the employees who are supposed to fill those roles and positions. Such practice makes talent management more strategic, as it has an impact on fulfilling an organisation's strategy and building its competitive advantage. It should be emphasised at this point that determining key positions and roles as well as filling them with high potential and high performers is determined by contextual factors including both the features of the organisation and the environment in which it operates.

Analysing the abundant literature on talent management makes it clear that the universalistic and managerial approach to talent management prevails, and the findings mainly concern large private companies including international and global entities (McDonnell et al., 2017). It is worth mentioning that the trend of international and global talent management is dynamically growing currently. It encompasses the whole set of activities and processes aimed at identifying, acquiring, developing and retaining talented employees on an international or global scale. Global talent management includes both universal elements of talent management and specific elements stemming from the context of the organisation's functioning on international markets as well as their specific nature. For example, cultural differences, relationships between different organisational entities of an international company, mergers and takeovers, as well as managing expatriates, may be listed as examples of additional issues broadening the scope of research and implementations within global talent management. Global talent management is often approached as a part of international HRM, though there are also many publications focusing entirely on issues of global talent management. Reviews of such papers are to be found, inter alia, in publications by McDonnell et al. (2017) and Purgał-Popiela (2018).

Frequent references to attaining high performance and improving an organisation's competitive advantage that occur with talent management are compliant with the resource-based view, according to which the sources of competitiveness are to be found in the specific and inimitable resources and competences of a company. The resources and competences are created in a process of complex interactions within the company as well as under the influence of external factors. They are time-consuming and highly dependent on the specific organisational context. From the perspective of talent management, the resource-based view focusses on collective social interactions rather than on the actions of an individual (Bowman & Hird, 2014).

Faced with increase in continuously changing environments, organisations may find it more and more difficult to determine in advance which resources and competences will be crucial for their competitiveness and thus how effective talent management programmes should be and which positions and employees should be addressed. In the changing, complex and unstable environment, keys to organisational success are openness to diversity, stimulating experience-based learning and entrepreneurial intuition (Bowman & Hird, 2014). In light of the above facts, new challenges emerge in talent management connected with redefining the existing paradigms/approaches to creating talent management policies and practices. The universalistic approach to the talent management process gives way to placing more emphasis on the specific context of organisational functioning. The assumption that it is mainly key employees/managers who have a strategic significance and that only they constitute the company's competitive advantage should be critically verified. When devising talent management programmes, the question arises of which individuals working for the organisation create value in contemporary as well as emerging business models. It seems justifiable to make talent management programmes open and available for different groups and individual employees and adjust them to the technical, organisational and cultural characteristics of organisations.

The approaches to talent management presented in professional literature and discussed above are mainly restricted to large companies, often multinationals of complex structures and formalised processes including HRM. Their applicability in particular organisations makes it necessary to consider the specific context of the companies' functioning. It also concerns small and medium enterprises, whose position in national economies, including Poland, is important. Knowing and improving HRM practices in general and especially those referring to talent management is essential for both researchers and managers. Unfortunately, this area seems to be under-researched thus far (Valverde et al., 2013; Sparrow et al., 2014; Festing et al., 2017). It is worth mentioning at this point what the main characteristics of small and medium enterprises are and why such companies cannot be treated as miniatures of larger enterprises (Pocztowski & Pauli, 2013). Small and medium enterprises have limited resources and market range, a lower level of strategy, structures as well as business process formalisation and a centralised, individual management style that is usually conducted by managers/owners; they also have not only a lower level of management professionalisation but also a high innovative potential and a fast reaction time to changes (Festing et al., 2017). Despite certain common features, it should be remembered that small and medium enterprises are, among other characteristics, diverse in terms of the number of employees when comparing micro, small and medium entities. Regardless of the differences, the specificity of SMEs and the context of their functioning affect HRM including talent management. There are two publications in which talent management in small and medium enterprises is thoroughly analysed. These present a qualitative study conducted in Spain (Valverde et al., 2013) and quantitative research performed in Germany (Festing et al., 2013). The third source of information used to investigate and determine the specificity of talent management in SMEs is research conducted by the authors of this book.

The research by Valverde et al. (2013) involved multiple case studies conducted on a group of six Spanish enterprises employing between 48 and 350 workers. It revealed that the managers are not familiar with the concepts of talent management or related formal management policies and practices; however, the respondents were able to identify talented individuals in their organisations. Most frequently, SMEs focus on performance and attitude rather than on potential when identifying talents. However, in defining talents' traits, the importance of dedication to the firm, motivation, loyalty, trust and responsibility is stressed. Employees identified as talents occupy diverse positions – most often of a managerial and specialist nature – but also other positions, which may even be basic. In HRM policy in the investigated SMEs, much attention is paid to the high level of competence among employees, with a particular emphasis on those occupying key positions as well as multitasking, which enables substituting other employees. Moreover, individuals identified as talents had longer work experience, during which they could prove their commitment, develop good interpersonal relationships with the managers and confirm their multitasking skills. The research did not prove the dominance of either the inclusive or the exclusive approach to talents in investigated SMEs. Although traits of both perspectives were present in the organisations, in enterprises where a more exclusive approach was observed, talents were privileged compared to other employees in terms of training as well as empowerment and independence at work, which caused a sense of injustice among other employees.

As mentioned above, the investigated companies identified talent in two ways: from the perspective of managerial and key positions, and from the perspective of all employees. The way in which talent is understood and approached impacts talent management policies and practices. In two cases, the egalitarian approach to talent management was observed, in which all employees were treated equally. In the first case, employees were regarded as talents; this resulted in continuous and broad investments in human capital, mainly in the form of business specific as well as general training. Workers could express their needs regarding training, which additionally made them perceive the dedicated training as a reward and care. In the second case, although all employees (excluding management) were treated equally, they were not regarded as talents but rather as a resource which may be exchanged/substituted and thus they were not invested in either in the form of training or other development and retention activities.

With regard to the enterprises in which talents were identified and thus the approach was rather elitist, there was a tendency to use the same HR tools for talents and other employees with the exception of some training courses in which talents were granted a greater number of hours. Nevertheless, the privileged attitude to talents was rather informal. There are two kinds of dedicated treatment of talented individuals: the first consists of a paternalistic management style which provides the group of talents with more privileged working hours, holidays, medical care or family support

programmes; the second is based on offering talents more possibilities to design tasks, access information and participate in the
decision-making process.

As far as other talent management practices are concerned,
it should be stated that the investigated enterprises showed only
limited activity with regard to talent acquisition, as they did not
claim to encounter difficulties with recruiting employees, despite
the common opinion in literature that it is a big challenge for small
and medium enterprises. There was no formal policy of retaining
employees either, with the exception of two companies which adopted the egalitarian approach and offered their employees a se-
niority bonus within their remuneration system. All the companies
from the research sample had some succession practices consisting
of identifying pivotal job positions, key employees occupying the
positions, but also their successors. Such practices did not concern
the post of the owner and managing director (Valverde et al., 2013).

The research findings prove that talent management practices are
executed in small and medium enterprises, even if the management
is not familiar with formal, theoretical concepts and terminology
in the field. The practices exhibit the previously discussed characteristics of different perspectives in defining talent and talent management. The research results showed that the category of small
and medium enterprises is not a homogeneous group and that it is
advisable to analyse medium and small entities separately.

The second study was conducted in 700 medium enterprises in
Germany. The sample comprised companies of up to 2000 employees. The research was quantitative in nature and had the form
of a questionnaire. The respondents were asked 24 questions that
were concerned with acquiring, selecting, developing and retaining
employees, as well as the companies' business context, referring in
particular to labour force shortages (Festing et al., 2013). The research made it possible to acquire an insight into applied HR practices and identify three approaches to talent management referred
to as clusters developed on the basis of the intensity of activities in
the field (Festing et al., 2017). The first cluster, referred to as *highly
engaged talent management*, comprised companies which implemented well-developed and complex talent management practices
and conducted them in a systematic manner. They made substan-
tial investments in employee training, applied measures to improve
their retention and to attract new workers. Such practices occurred
mostly in the group of the largest companies within the research
sample. The second cluster, called *reactive talent management*,

included companies which focussed mainly on HR planning. Their aim was talent acquisition and identification and they executed only limited activity with regard to employee training and retention. The third approach referred to as *retention-based talent management* applied to companies which focussed mainly on developing, career planning and motivating talented employees in order to retain them. Practices connected with recruitment and selection were peripheral in these companies.

The investigated companies used an inclusive approach to talent management, addressing talent management activities with regard to all employees. It has been confirmed that the organisations took advantage of cooperation and networking to improve their talent management practices. The activities focussed mainly on talent retention and investing in the development of talented individuals, which was imposed by shortages on the labour market. The role of managers and owners in the activities was crucial. Less attention was paid to searching new sources of recruiting talents or managing diversity. There were also some deficits in strategic thinking concerning talent management in investigated enterprises. Additionally, it turned out that despite the specificity of small and medium enterprises including HRM, there was a tendency to copy talent management practices from large entities. This may be caused by the fact that in the war for talent, SMEs want to offer similar solutions to their larger competitors (Festing et al., 2013).

The results of the research conducted by the authors of this book are discussed in detail in the next chapter. The research sample consisted of 200 small and medium enterprises operating in Poland who executed talent management activities. The findings indicate that talent is, in most cases, viewed as unique competences; it is approached from both the inclusive and exclusive perspective, and talent management activities are addressed to employees occupying specialist, executive and managerial positions. Besides the commonly available development programmes for all talented employees, there are extraordinary solutions regarding remuneration, appraisal and career building (Pocztowski et al., 2019).

Despite some limitations stemming from the diversity of research samples, the tools applied by the authors, and the different contexts in which the studies were conducted, the above-mentioned examples of studies in the field of talent management definitely contribute to improving knowledge concerning TM practices and policies in small and medium enterprises and confirm the specificity and uniqueness of SMEs compared to large organisations. This specificity is expressed, inter alia, by the strong influence of contextual factors concerning cultural characteristics, legal solutions and the condition of the labour market. Different forms of doing business and the diversity of small and medium enterprises lead to a variety of approaches to defining talent and performing talent management. To sum up, the opinions concerning talent management in small and medium enterprises expressed in the literature seem to overlap with previous research findings (Krishan & Scullion, 2017) constituting a reference point for further in-depth studies of the issue, which the authors strongly recommend. A multinational research project conducted in compliance with a common homogeneous procedure would enable the elimination of certain constraints characteristic of separate studies.

## Talent as a Source of Competitive Advantage

Talent management may be analysed with a different level of details, which is reflected in Wiblen and McDonnell's (2019) classification. The researchers indicated four levels on which talent management can be analysed: micro (referring to an individual), mezzo (connected with the location of the organisation or department in which the person works), macro (embracing the whole organisation) and meta (referring to the social and institutional context). Taking into account the considerations presented in the previous part of the book, the classification may be made with the inclusion of a particular field of science upon which the discussion concerning talent and talent management is based. At the level of an individual, talent is analysed mainly from the point of view of psychological sciences; at the organisation level, it is analysed from the perspective of management studies. Approaching talent in the context of the whole country, it may be analysed from the perspective of economics.

At each of the levels, talent may be a source of competitive advantage. For an individual, talent determines employability on the labour market, so it ensures them a highly competitive position compared with other candidates. For an organisation, talent affects its business outcome and creates its market potential. For the whole country, the number of talents and their performance may influence macroeconomic indicators concerning, for example, GDP, growth dynamics and the innovativeness level of the economy; thus, talented individuals establish the country's position in the international arena. Regarding talent as a source of competitiveness at the three levels is supported by Schultz's research findings, according to which people make an important contribution to the wealth of nations, as they possess certain components of human capital such as knowledge, skills, predispositions and health, which determine both the quantity and quality of work (Schultz, 1961).

### *National Level*

The impact of talents on the competitive position of particular countries may be analysed on the basis of the findings of the Global Talent Competitiveness Index (GTCI; Lanvin & Monteiro, 2019) report. Its authors proved a strong correlation between the level of per capita income and the effectiveness of talent management in particular countries. Furthermore, they revealed that the gap in talent between countries of high and low income has increased over the last few years (Lanvin & Monteiro, 2019, p. VII). The major axis of analyses presented in the report from 2019 is entrepreneurial talent, which denotes a combination of creativity, innovation, flexibility, adaptability, risk-taking and energy needed to achieve success on the market and undertake necessary measures in the ever-changing environment (Lanvin & Monteiro, 2019, p. VII). According to the authors, entrepreneurial talent reveals itself not only in the context of a micro organisation, but also in large multinationals, which compete on global markets. It should be stated though that this specific kind of (entrepreneurial) talent is particularly significant in small and medium enterprises, where the owner, managing director or a person occupying a pivotal position makes most decisions referring to the direction of activities the organisation undertakes.

Entrepreneurial talent should be analysed in the context of the whole socio-economic system of a given country, as only the solutions on the level of national economy will bring about a leverage effect in which individuals' potential will contribute to growth and development. Talent management at this level should embrace proper regulations: legal (increasing the organisation's freedom of action), economic (providing access to financial resources), educational (to provide new knowledge and popularise and promote new solutions) and social (supporting open mindedness, creativity and innovativeness).

Bearing in mind the above considerations, it should be acknowledged that the following factors, referring to four areas discussed below, will affect the possibility to use talents at the national level: factors providing landscape for effective performance (Enable), factors attracting talents (Attract), factors providing development opportunities (Grow) and retaining factors (Retain).

The first group encompasses legal and systemic solutions in a given country as well as the market- and sector-specific situation. The condition on the labour market determining employees' availability and their competences is also important.

'Attract' activities refer to, among other factors, supporting foreign direct investments, which stimulate international cooperation and increase the availability of financial resources and activities aimed at obtaining high-skilled foreigners, which will provide new knowledge.

Growing talents refers to creating opportunities and prospects for development, which include activities upgrading competences by both formal education and other forms of improving skills and knowledge.

The last element focuses on providing talents with such a quality of life that they do not need to look for better prospects overseas.

In the GTCI rankings, Poland is in the 42nd position with the score of 47.41 out of 100 points. Table 2.1 presents the highest- and lowest-ranked factors.

*Table 2.1* Poland's profile in GTCI report

| Factor group | Positively ranked criteria | Negatively ranked criteria |
| --- | --- | --- |
| Enable | • Ease of doing business<br>• Low corruption<br>• ICT infrastructure | • Business–government relations<br>• Ease of hiring<br>• Labour–employer cooperation |
| Attract | • FDI and technology transfer<br>• Tolerance of minorities<br>• Female graduates | • Ease of finding skilled employees<br>• Tolerance of immigrants<br>• Leadership opportunities for women |
| Grow | • Formal education<br>• Vocational enrolment<br>• Tertiary enrolment | • Collaboration across organisations<br>• Collaboration within organisations<br>• Delegation of authority |
| Retain | • Pension system<br>• Social protection<br>• Sanitation | • Social protection<br>• Brain retention<br>• Physician density |

On the basis of the above data, it may be stated that activities aimed at acquiring and retaining highly qualified workers greatly impact the number of talents in Poland. Although various forms of improving competences are easily available, activities regarding talent retention attained quite low scores and acquiring talented individuals from abroad attained very low ranks. The findings suggest that a part of the measures undertaken within investment in human capital is not redistributed in the form of talents' performance as some decide to work abroad.

### Organisation Level

The significance of talent management programmes for organisational competitiveness may be analysed from a broader perspective including the importance of HR practices for business success. One of the basic approaches to analysing this interdependence assumes that appropriate HRM enables the attaining of positive outcomes that may be classified into one of three categories: financial, organisational and HRM outcomes. It should be indicated at this point that such a relationship might be reciprocal. The research conducted by Shin and Konrad (2017) and Roca-Puig, Bou-Llusar, Beltran-Martin and Garcia-Juan (2019) proved that the quality of HR practices has a positive influence on a company's performance, which leads to gaining presumed benefits. This, in turn, provides the company with a greater pool of assets and broadens its organisational, relational and material resources, which are later used to improve HRM processes. Modified personnel processes support attaining new and more complex purposes, which guarantees even greater performance. Additionally, the quality of HR practices improves employee performance, as adequately designed and implemented HR processes encourage employees to take initiative and be creative with regard to enhancing their organisation's functioning (Khoreva & Wechtler, 2018).

Although the majority of associations occurring between HR processes and organisational performance as well as building competitive potential has been investigated and described using studies of large organisations, the correlation also exists in small and medium enterprises. Research conducted by Patel and Cardon (2010) proved that implementing proper HR practices positively impacts upon SMEs' competitiveness. The correlation refers to, inter alia, increasing the level of SMEs' credibility, which helps acquire better qualified workers. Additionally, small entities are more reliant on employees' competences, as their access to other resources (financial, material) is limited. This is why competing on the market, they focus on the commitment, creativity, knowledge and skills of their employees. Sheehan's (2014) research indicated that proper HR practices concerning remuneration, competence developing opportunities and strategic aspects of HRM are directly connected with SMEs' financial outcomes. The dependence has also been proven by Rauch and Hatak (2016), who proved that HR practices impact upon the financial and organisational outcomes of SMEs, and their findings show that the quality of personnel process in small and medium enterprises may have a greater impact on SMEs' performance rather than on the performance of large entities.

Based on the interdependence between HRM processes and organisational performance, it may be stated that talent management as a subarea of HRM will have a great influence on an organisation's competitiveness. The correlation stems, on the one hand, from the significance of talents' attributes for the organisation, and on the other, from the quality and organisation of processes, practices and activities conducted within talent management. In the first case, the resource-based view (Barney, 1991) should be used as a theoretical basis; in the second case, the concept of strategic (dynamic) capabilities of an organisation should be adopted.

When talent is defined as a person having inborn, unique abilities and/or above-average skills and expert knowledge, the attributes make a specific human capital, which is inherently irreplaceable and inimitable. The uniqueness of such components is perceived by companies as particularly valuable and leads to the achievement of an organisation's strategic goals. Additionally, talents' skills and abilities may be promoted by a company's organisational capital, which will enable the organisation to reach substantially higher performance in its financial, relational and intra-organisational aspects (Sparrow & Makram, 2015). The human capital of talented individuals contributes to attaining more benefits or even to the synergy effect resulting from interaction between human, organisational and relational capital. This combination is different and unique in each organisation and thus it may constitute a source of competitive advantage for a company on the market.

Dynamic capabilities are inner practices and activity schemes that make it possible to acquire, blend and take advantage of a company's resources in order to achieve strategic goals. They enable modifications of a company's functioning and responding to the changes that may occur on the market. Dynamic capabilities are unique processes created during organisational development, which enable their perception as a source of a company's competitive advantage (Eisenhardt & Martin, 2000). In accordance with this theory, Sparrow and Makram (2015) indicated that talent management (as a process) has an effect on and is affected by other HRM activities (e.g. gaining knowledge, sharing knowledge and cooperating). For this reason, implementing and conducting effective talent management may itself become a source of a company's competitiveness. This stems from the fact that talent management is defined as a process of systematic identification of pivotal positions in an organisation and filling them with high potentials and high performers. Furthermore, it is necessary to implement such HRM activities as to boost talent development and commitment (Collings & Mellahi, 2009). To achieve the presumed goals, organisations have to create a unique system providing talents access to a company's resources as well as enabling identification, coding and implementing both the existing knowledge and the newly created knowledge by talents (Sparrow & Makram, 2015). The quality of applied talent management programmes is critical for the degree of the company's advantages. The research also proved that the way in which talents perceive the activities dedicated for them affects initiatives regarding improving competences and the level of talents' involvement. The quality of programmes refers to how talents define and assess their psychological contract with the company they work for. The more comprehensive and successful talent management programmes are, the higher rank talents give to the organisation's commitment, which results in a greater performance and motivation of this group of workers (Khoreva, Vaiman & Van Zalk, 2017).

The literature review conducted by Bethke-Langenger et al. (2011) confirmed that organisations having a precisely defined talent management strategy attain higher financial outcomes than other entities. This mainly refers to profit level, sales, productivity, the margin and the value for shareholders. With regards to the organisational dimension, companies that manage talents are more efficient, their internal processes are more professional and they are better at assessing the market potential. Regarding human resources, talent management practices positively impact employees' involvement, competence improvement, developing career paths and limiting employee turnover. The correlation between talent management programmes and the above-mentioned categories has been positively verified in empirical studies conducted on a group of 580 organisations (Bethke-Langenger et al., 2011). The signifi-cance of appropriately designed talent management systems has been proven by Jiang, Lepak, Hu and Baer (2012). They used the AMO (*ability-motivation-opportunity*) model to show that activities supporting the three elements (developing knowledge and skills, in-creasing motivation and providing opportunities to take advantage of the competences) positively impact upon a company's financial and organisational outcomes. This confirmed Collings and Mellahi's (2009) findings, according to which a company's perfor-mance is closely connected with talents' motivation to work, ded-ication and undertaking activities that go beyond their standard responsibilities. The authors claim that strengthening the three areas is critical to make the best of talents' unique characteristics.

As a result of the above, it may be stated that talent management enables the creation of the competitive potential of organisations. On the one hand, it results from the fact that talented individuals have specific components of human capital that constitute value for an organisation. On the other hand, properly designed processes (aimed at acquiring, developing, motivating, remunerating and re-taining talents) may be treated as a strategic capability distinguish-ing the company from its competitors. The specificity of small and medium enterprises (revealed in, among other factors, their diver-sity, different business models and a more limited availability of fi-nancial and material resources compared with large organisations) cause the right design of talent management processes to be vital for the company's competitiveness.

### *Individual Level*

At the level of an individual, talent issues should be considered in the context of employability. This means analysing the degree to which characteristics allowing someone to be regarded as a talent influences their chances to find the right job, which is a job that will generate expected return on investment in human capital. According to van der Heijde and van der Heiden's (2006) concept, employabil-ity consists of five dimensions: occupational expertise, anticipation and optimisation, which entails preparing for future changes on the labour market, personal flexibility, adaptability to the requirements of the company and eagerness to perform diversified roles, as well as maintaining balance in the compromise between one's own work and career interests and organisational goals. Based on their findings, the authors confirmed that a high level of employability is positively correlated with developing a career path, performance on current job positions, long-term work outcomes and the performance of the organisations a given employee is working for. In their conclusions, they also indicated that the level of employability may be dependent upon the individual predispositions, capabilities and personality of an employee – which are the constituents of talent defining criteria. Nilsson and Ellstrom (2012) came up with similar findings. They defined employability as a set of competences and individual features that are critical to fulfil the requirements of the dynamically changing and competitive labour market. They claim that such an approach is convergent with the existing definitions of talent, but the term employability is broader and talent is its key component.

When analysing employability, it should be indicated that such factors as expert knowledge, skills, attitudes and predispositions affect its level. Additionally, employees' individual contacts/acquaintances and interpersonal relationships that they can take advantage of at work also have a great importance. The above factors overlap with those presented previously in the section devoted to different approaches to talent and its dimensions. Thus, if an individual has an above-average potential expressed in the form of professional expertise or a master's degree in some area and, additionally, they have exceptional abilities and predispositions, their employability will be high. This is conducive to a highly competitive position of talented individuals on the labour market, as many organisations will strive to hire such candidates.

## Theoretical Model of Talent Management in Small and Medium Enterprises

As previously mentioned, according to the literature review, talent management in SMEs has some peculiarities resulting from lack of resources, reactive management practices and the lack of formalised processes (Festing et al., 2017). It is also not a kind of miniaturisation of talent management used in large companies, which makes use of existing talent management models rather limited. With consideration to all the above facts, a theoretical model has been developed by the authors (see Figure 2.2), which assumes that talent management practices are influenced by contextual factors as well as by the owners' mindset, and they have an impact on business, organisational and HR-related outcomes.

To implement talent management policies and practices in SMEs, appropriate conditions must be created under which employees'

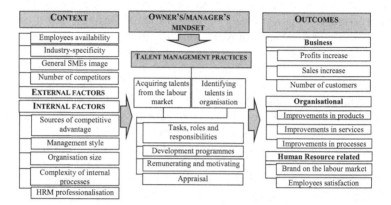

*Figure 2.2* Theoretical model of talent management in small and medium enterprises.

potential can be identified, used in accordance with the firm's requirements and developed in order to meet strategic goals. Such conditions are influenced by both external and internal factors. External factors may refer to the general market situation or they might be industry-specificity. From the wide range of factors that may influence the ability to introduce talent management practices, the following four seem to have the highest importance:

- employees' availability,
- industry-specificity,
- general image of SMEs,
- number of competitors.

In the group of internal factors that seem to have the most significant impact on talent management practices in SMEs are:

- sources of competitive advantage,
- management style,
- organisation size,
- complexity of internal processes,
- HRM professionalisation level.

The second component of the theoretical model consists of the specification of talent management practices resulting from owners' values and attitudes towards talents; this component determines how contextual factors are perceived. Contextual factors will narrow and structure activities taken by SMEs in order to achieve optimal effects on human capital. They will help decide whether to *identify talents* and develop the specified group of employees or to *acquire* them from the labour market. They will shape the *scope of tasks, roles and responsibilities* and provide information to be used in designing *development programmes*. The attitude to talent management will result in implementing *remuneration* and *motivation systems*. Both of these should strengthen the psychological contract and build talents' commitment. The whole system should also include special *appraisal* procedures that will allow evaluation of competences and assess performance. All these practices should provide appropriate person–organisation fit that will prevent employee turnover and enable reaching the desired effects.

The outcomes of introducing talent management activities can be divided into three categories: *business, organisational* and *HR-related*. Acquiring highly skilled candidates, developing employees' competences and creating motivational systems are mostly aimed at enhancing commitment, and raising profits, sales value and the number of customers. Because talent management practices increase the value of human capital, it may also result in higher innovativeness of a particular SME. Such an organisation will introduce new products and services or may improve them in accordance with customer expectations. Possible effects of talent management programmes may also touch upon SMEs' internal systems. Such organisations change or widen their internal systems as a result of new knowledge acquisition. The last category of outcomes corresponds to the image of SMEs on the internal as well as the external labour market. Organisations that value talents and introduce appropriate talent management practices are perceived as those creating better and customised work environments. Thus, they more often become an employer of choice. Moreover, having the possibility to participate in talent management programmes increases employees' satisfaction, which helps to retain talents, strengthen their organisational commitment and leads to higher performance.

The developed theoretical model describes an approach to talent management in SMEs that focusses on employer branding and employee value proposition, the acquisition of high potential and highly qualified candidates, the optimisation of rotation and retention rates and the development of key competences. The scope of activities taken in such firms will differ in accordance with both external and internal contextual factors, which will result in achieving outcomes that can be divided, as previously mentioned, into three general categories: business performance, organisational improvements and HR-related improvements.

Talent management practices enable the optimal use of employees' competences, which, according to the resource-based view of the firm (Barney, 1991, Pike, Roos & Marr, 2005), can build competitive advantage on the basis of human capital. Thus, SMEs that introduce talent management practices achieve a higher level of business performance, which can be measured by means of sales value and volume, profits and the number of customers.

## Notes

1  The main studies in this trend focus on two major issues: early identification of talented individuals (childhood) and the specificity of supporting talented kids in the literacy classroom. The differentiated model of giftedness and talent (DMGT) by Gagné stems from this trend. It shows how one's natural abilities (gift) in four domains (intellectual, creative, socio-affective, sensorimotor) may or may not be transferred into systematically developed skills in seven fields of human life: academics, arts, business, leisure, social actions, sports and technology (Gagné, 2004).

2  The difference is evident. Competences mean mastery, the outcome of which is located somewhere between the minimal acceptable level and significantly above the average level; while a talented employee's performance is in the top 10% of the highest performance within a given domain (Gagnè, 2000).

3  However, the question of distinguishing between talent management and strategic human resource management is a key issue. According to this interpretation, talent management becomes a set of typical personnel processes in an organisation (Collings & Mellahi, 2009; Silzer & Dowell, 2010).

# 3 Context of Talent Management in Small and Medium Enterprises

According to Gallardo-Gallardo et al. (2019), there is a growing consensus regarding the application of a 'best-fit' approach to talent management and the inclusion of contextual factors as they shape the practices and scope of actions undertaken by organisations. To implement talent management programmes in SMEs, appropriate conditions must be created under which employees' potential can be identified, which is used in accordance with the firm's requirements and developed in order to meet the organisation's strategic goals. Such conditions are influenced by both external and internal factors (Gallardo-Gallardo et al. 2019). External factors either refer to general market situation and institutional pressures or are industry-specific. In some research, the external context is also investigated in a wider perspective including global market dynamics (Vaiman, Sparrow, Schuler & Collings, 2018) or differences between country markets (Thunnissen & Gallardo-Gallardo, 2019). Internal factors include mission, vision, strategy, leadership, culture, systems, processes and structure (Thunnissen & Gallardo-Gallardo, 2017, p. 114). In this study, the external and internal factors were divided into the following nine categories in order to capture their potential impact upon talent management practices in SMEs:

*External*: employee availability, industry specificity, general image of SME, number of competitors.
*Internal*: sources of competitive advantage, management style, organisation size, complexity of internal processes, HRM professionalisation level.

*Employee availability* refers to the number of occupationally active people in the country or region in which a particular SME operates. Availability can be estimated by both quantitative means (the number of occupationally active people in a particular labour market) and qualitative means (the level of competences and potential of occupationally active people). The specifics of the local labour market can have an impact upon the design of talent management practices. For example, a shortage of skilled workers makes companies invest more in the development of identified talents and introduce activities aimed at retaining them. By contrast, in markets where there is wide pool of potentially talented candidates, firms may focus on attracting and selecting suitable candidates among them.

*Industry specificity* refers to the ratio between general and firm-specific knowledge, skills and attitudes. In some industries, companies may achieve an appropriate level of performance on the basis of general competences; in other industries, specialised knowledge or skills are crucial for survival and growth. Industry characteristics may also influence the willingness of potential employees to work for a particular organisation.

*General image of SME* refers to the perception of the given SME as an employer of choice. In a particular country or region in which large or even multinational companies have a high share in employment, SMEs may not be perceived as valuable employers. It is commonly believed that large companies provide employees with a wider range of benefits, developmental and career opportunities, a higher salary and work security. On such labour markets, qualified employees would rather choose to work for large companies, which limits SMEs' pool of valuable candidates. According to Thunnissen, Boselie and Fruytier (2013), organisations should pay great attention to their brand as employers and implement marketing tools to identify key competitors. These will result in, for example, creating specified employee value propositions for talents.

*The number of competitors* not only affects labour demand but also the level of HRM practice professionalisation and the scope of incentives and benefits that are offered by employers. By analysing trends on the labour market in European Union (EU) countries, it can be stated that SMEs face increasing difficulties in hiring employees that have appropriate competences. There is a decreasing number of young people entering the labour market, expectations of the required competences are rising and the number of large competitors is increasing.

*Sources of competitive advantage* refers to both tangible and intangible assets (Barney, 1991; Galbreath, 2005; Pike et al., 2005). Organisations that focus on tangible resources will pay much more attention to machinery, buildings and assets. In such organisations, the focus on human capital is lower, which affects the number of actions undertaken in order to hire highly qualified employees or develop their competences. By contrast, firms aimed at building competitive advantage on the basis of intangible assets will pay much more attention to relational, organisational and human capital. This makes these organisation focus on employee competences, which may result in a willingness to introduce TM programmes.

*Management style* refers to the extent to which employees may participate in designing the course of their company's action and take responsibility for the way they fulfil their tasks. The less directive the managerial style is, the more opportunity employees have to develop their competences and use their potential.

*Organisation size* influences the scope of talent management programmes and the introduction of specific practices. For example, in small organisations there is no possibility to build a vertical career due to the number of levels within the structure. Moreover, it is impossible to organise firm-specific training in such organisations using group learning techniques because there are not enough participants. In most cases, small firms have to limit building career paths to those that are focused on competences and roles. They prefer to apply individual learning techniques or external training in development programmes. The organisation size also has an impact on the number of actors involved in talent management. Despite the fact that in the model of Thunissen and Gallardo-Gallardo (2017, p. 114), top managers, HR specialists and employees are included, in small organisations it can be narrowed down to only the owner and an employee.

Taking into account *internal processes*, it can be stated that their variety will require a wider scope of competences. This causes a necessity to hire employees with interdisciplinary knowledge and more complex skills and provide them with opportunities to acquire new skills. Thus, organisations in which various and complex processes are run may pay more attention to talent development, while those in which processes are narrow and simple may focus mainly on attracting talented workers.

*The level of HRM professionalisation* has a direct influence upon the structure of talent management programmes. The lack of an HRM system in an organisation results in difficulties with implementing practices for employees with high potential and competence levels.

## External Factors

### *Employees Availability*

There are two main factors relating to labour market conditions that may have an impact upon talent management practices. The first is the number of occupationally active people and the second is the requirements that potential employees are supposed to fulfil. Thus, the respondents were asked to evaluate how they perceive the availability of potential employees and whether they set any specific requirements with regard to candidates' competences.

The data gathered (see Table 3.1) shows that more than half of respondents (57%) find it difficult to hire employees in specialist positions. Only 12% claim they do not face any problems with finding candidates with an expected level of competences. Such opinions reflect a general situation on the labour market, due to which companies claim to have problems with the recruitment of highly qualified workers.

Interestingly, one out of every four SMEs does not define any specific requirements with regard to the competences of candidates (see Table 3.2). Half of the respondents claim they occasionally search for employees with some specific competences adjusted to tasks or processes run in the organisation. Thus, it can be assumed that general competences, which are also considered to be valuable in other companies, form the basis of the candidate selection process. Only 2% of the investigated SMEs stated that they have precisely defined expectations and requirements regarding candidates' competences; these refer to the uniqueness of tasks and internal processes.

An analysis of data gathered did not support potential interdependence between employee availability and the level of requirements towards competences. This means that in the investigated group of SMEs, difficulties in hiring employees do not stem from defining requirements that are too high.

*Table 3.1* Employee availability

|  | Share in % |
| --- | --- |
| There is a deficiency of candidates that may occupy basic positions | 19.50 |
| There is a deficiency of candidates that may occupy specialist positions | 57.00 |
| There is a deficiency of candidates that may occupy managerial positions | 11.50 |
| We have no problems with finding candidates that meet our expectations | 12.00 |

*Table 3.2* Requirements towards candidates' competences

|  | Share in % |
|---|---|
| We have not defined any specific requirements regarding candidates' competences. | 23.00 |
| We occasionally define some requirements that refer to unique processes or tasks. | 50.50 |
| We have defined requirements to a large extent; we run many unique processes that require a set of specific competences. | 24.50 |
| We have defined requirements to a very large extent; in our company unique and crafted processes are dominant, thus specific competences are precisely defined. | 2.00 |

### *Industry Specificity*

Due to the fact that SMEs operate in various industries, their specificity may impact the design of talent management practices. Thus, the investigated companies were questioned about the level of sector development and about key factors impacting organisation growth in this industry.

On the basis of the gathered data, it can be stated that activities aimed at talent management are mostly introduced in emerging or niche sectors (see Table 3.3). Only one out of every three companies declared that it operates in well-developed sectors in which there is a high level of competition.

In well-developed sectors, the market position of SMEs stems mostly from the low level of costs, the company brand and product/service quality as they have to compete with other SMEs as well as with large organisations. Thus, employees' potential and competences may not be perceived as a primary factor in building a competitive advantage. In niche sectors, some specific, precisely targeted products and services are offered. This results in the need to hire and

*Table 3.3* Industry specificity

|  | Share in % |
|---|---|
| A well-developed sector with many competitors | 33.00 |
| A well-developed niche sector with only a few competitors | 46.00 |
| An emerging sector which will develop and increase its market share | 17.50 |
| An emerging niche sector which will develop, but the market share will remain stable | 3.50 |

*Table 3.4* Factors impacting firms' potential to grow

|  | Share in % |
|---|---|
| Experience | 53.50 |
| Price | 47.00 |
| Brand | 41.00 |
| Innovativeness | 35.00 |
| Knowledge | 32.00 |
| Natural resources availability | 30.00 |
| Quality | 30.00 |
| Machinery and technology | 28.00 |
| Closeness to customers | 28.00 |
| Logistics and supply chain | 18.00 |

*Note*: Respondents could choose any applicable.

retain a unique group of employees with a specific set of knowledge, skills and abilities that may be perceived as talent indicators.

Among the factors affecting SMEs' potential for growth, experience (53.5%), price level (47.5%) and brand (41%), were most often selected (see Table 3.4). These factors do not directly refer to the importance of human capital, which is assigned to be the foundation of implementing talent management. However, these factors imply the importance of intangible resources. The experience of firms and their brands are the components of organisational capital developed over the course of the lifetime of the organisations. Factors that directly refer to human capital – innovativeness and knowledge – were selected by approximately one out of every three companies.

Interestingly, the investigated companies do not consider tangible resources to be of high importance. Less than one out of every three companies claimed that the potential to grow depends on: natural resource availability; machinery and technology; proximity to customers (firm's location). Thus, it can be concluded that due to the digitisation level, the infrastructure improvement, the distance between customers and the suppliers and firm's location are neither obstacles in running a business nor factors enhancing competitive position.

### Image of SMEs

SMEs compete on the labour market with other organisations. Thus, the general image these companies have as employers may impact the shape and scope of talent management practices. The specificity of SMEs (referring to simple organisational structures, flexibility, owners' roles and informal relationships) may be perceived as an advantage by some employees and as a disadvantage by others. In general,

SMEs tend to be regarded as companies, which offer a relatively low salary, and reduced opportunities to develop competences and promotion prospects. Thus, SMEs are not identified as employers of choice by many talented candidates.

To explore how these organisations are perceived on the labour market, respondents were asked to indicate to what extent the answers listed in Table 3.5 apply to SME image.

Based on the gathered data, it can be concluded that in general the respondents perceive SMEs as valuable employers. More than 70% of them agreed with all the listed statements. Of all the statements, that which referred to friendly relationships was most frequently highlighted. Approximately four out of every five emphasised SMEs' flexibility. In the respondents' opinion, SMEs are

*Table 3.5* General image of SMEs on the labour market

| | Share in % | | | | |
|---|---|---|---|---|---|
| | *Definately disagree* | *Rather disagree* | *Rather agree* | *Definately agree* | *Do not know, hard to say* |
| As companies in which relationships are friendly | 6.50 | 10.50 | 44.00 | 36.50 | 2.50 |
| As flexible employers, adjusting to employees' expectations | 3.50 | 11.00 | 51.50 | 27.50 | 6.50 |
| As companies providing employees with an opportunity to achieve work–life balance | 6.00 | 10.50 | 48.00 | 28.00 | 7.50 |
| As companies in which varied projects are run | 6.50 | 13.00 | 46.00 | 29.50 | 5.00 |
| As companies offering interesting jobs, adjusted to employee competences | 9.00 | 12.50 | 41.50 | 33.50 | 3.50 |
| As companies offering attractive working terms and conditions | 5.00 | 17.00 | 41.50 | 32.50 | 4.00 |
| As companies offering a competitive salary | 5.50 | 14.00 | 45.50 | 28.00 | 7.00 |
| As companies providing employees with competence development opportunities | 5.00 | 19.50 | 45.50 | 27.50 | 2.50 |

capable of adjusting to employees' expectations and provide them with opportunities to achieve work–life balance. Task-related issues were also often selected. Three out of every four respondents believe that in SMEs, one can take part in varied projects and fulfil interesting competence-adjusted tasks.

The lowest share of respondents agreed with statements that SMEs offer a competitive salary and competence development opportunities. This opinion is in line with the general image of SMEs on the labour market.

Such an image of SMEs on the labour market should attract talents. However, relatively low opportunities for competence development may be perceived as a real disadvantage. It should also be stated that this image is based on the subjective opinions of owners or managers and may differ from the opinion of employees, especially in the case of young workers.

### Market Competitiveness

Firms operating in highly competitive environments may expect that acquiring talents will result in both the introduction of innovations in products or services offered and in the development of internal processes. These should result in increasing income, lowering costs and improving the overall financial condition of the given firm. The analysis of the number of competitors shows that the investigated companies operate on markets with moderate competition. Approximately one out of every five SMEs declared to have more than 20 competitors on both the local and regional markets; every third firm claimed they have the same number of competitors on the domestic market, but 38% of investigated companies have to compete with more than 20 competitors on international markets (see Table 3.6).

Interestingly, 45% of investigated SMEs declared they have only one to three competitors on international markets. This may result

*Table 3.6* Market competition

| Activity range | Number of competitors (share in %) | | | |
|---|---|---|---|---|
| | 1–3 | 4–10 | 10–20 | More than 20 |
| Local | 38.00 | 20.00 | 22.00 | 20.00 |
| Regional | 19.50 | 34.50 | 24.50 | 21.50 |
| Domestic | 16.00 | 24.00 | 27.00 | 33.00 |
| International | 45.00 | 14.50 | 2.50 | 38.00 |

from the industry or sector specificity in which they operate. As previously discussed, the highest share of investigated companies (49.5%) operate in niche or in emerging sectors (17%).

Linking the area within which firms operate with the number of competitors on the market, it can be concluded that SMEs operating on local markets face the highest competition from companies that operate nationwide. More than half (53%) of locally operating companies have more than 20 country-level competitors. For firms offering their products or services on regional, domestic and international markets, the main threat comes from international companies. As many as 32% of regionally, 40% of nationally and 42% of internationally operating SMEs have more than 20 competitors operating on international markets.

## Internal Factors

### *Sources of Competitive Advantage*

To identify determinants enabling the creation of the competitive potential of the investigated SMEs, respondents were asked to indicate factors that refer to the main resource classifications: tangible assets, human capital, relational capital and organisational capital (see Table 3.7).

*Table 3.7* Sources of competitive advantage

| | *Share in %* | | | | |
|---|---|---|---|---|---|
| | *To a very high extent* | *To a high extent* | *To a low extent* | *To a very low extent* | *Does not impact upon* |
| Innovativeness | 30.0 | 53.5 | 11.5 | 4.5 | 0.5 |
| Time to react to changes | 25.0 | 55.0 | 15.0 | 3.4 | 0.5 |
| Closeness to markets/ customers | 30.0 | 48.0 | 15.0 | 5.5 | 1.5 |
| Competences and know-how | 29.0 | 49.0 | 15.5 | 6.0 | 0.5 |
| Price of products/services | 34.5 | 41.5 | 19.0 | 4.0 | 1.0 |
| Quality of products/services | 45.0 | 31.0 | 16.5 | 7.0 | 0.5 |
| Location | 23.0 | 53.0 | 18.0 | 6.5 | 0.5 |
| Customer service standards | 24.0 | 49.5 | 16.5 | 10.0 | 0.0 |
| Brand | 27.0 | 45.5 | 18.0 | 8.5 | 1.0 |
| Technology and machinery | 25.5 | 45.5 | 17.0 | 60 | 6.0 |
| Logistics and supply chain | 19.0 | 49.0 | 17.0 | 11.5 | 3.5 |
| Natural resource availability | 17.0 | 44.5 | 22.5 | 11.0 | 5.0 |
| Others | 0.5 | 4.0 | 18.0 | 13.5 | 64.0 |

The results of the conducted analysis show that *innovativeness* and *time-to-react to changes* were identified as primary factors. Of the investigated SMEs, 83.5% claimed that innovativeness and 80% that time-to-react have an impact upon the competitive advantage to a very high or a high extent. Both these factors strongly rely on human as well as on organisational capital, as employee competences and internal processes enable change and innovation. Thus, it can be concluded that talent management practices are aimed at making optimal use of employees' potential in order to introduce creative solutions in a dynamic business environment.

The following statements, taken from the qualitative research, illustrate sources of competitive advantage (see Box 3.1).

---

**BOX 3.1  SOURCES OF COMPETITIVE ADVANTAGE**

The main source of competitive advantage is human capital as well as equipment and software, which does not exist in other companies. (Company R)

The most important is the relationship with customers and a unique approach to each client. (Company A)

A fresh team which does not exist in other companies. (Company K)

Experience on the market (we have operated in the sector for over 20 years), advanced products and services adjusted to customers' needs and their loyalty. (Company P)

The key source of competitive advantage is people (employees). The one who hires highly qualified specialists who are also dedicated and have the same values and attitudes will win the market game. (Company E)

The most important is quality of products and services. We sell our products on international markets, and that is why we have to keep balance between the price and quality continuously, but the quality is the key factor. (Company O)

Flexibility and time to react to changes. The fact that we are able to adjust to market trends and conditions, and that we can anticipate them, builds our advantage. The second factor is an effective team, which consists of people sharing the same values and goals is highly engaged in running a business. (Company J)

---

According to the gathered data, factors referring to tangible assets exert the lowest impact upon firms' competitiveness. As many as 71% of the respondents highlighted technology and machinery as factors that impact upon firm competitiveness to a very high or high extent. The same importance was attributed by 61.5% to natural resource availability and to logistics and the supply chain. It can be concluded that tangible resources are crucial in production or delivering services, but they do not create competitive potential.

### Management Style

To identify how SMEs are managed, four areas were investigated. The first relates to the decision-making process, the second concerns job design, the third refers to the organisational structure and the level of its formalisation and the last concerns the assessment of the relationships between employees in particular SMEs.

Information provided by the respondents shows that the decision-making process in their organisations is highly centralised. In 22.5% of cases, it is only the owner/manager who defines goals and controls their effects. In these SMEs, employees are not involved in discussing decisions. In more than half of the organisations (52%), decisions are made by the owner/manager and employees may communicate or consult them to specify or modify both goals and the ways of achieving them. Only 6.5% respondents claimed that the owner/manager and employees make decisions jointly. Such an approach was implemented in order to develop employee competences and increase their involvement as well as their responsibility with regard to the firm's functioning.

Employees' duties are precisely defined in less than one out of four companies (23%). This means that in these companies, job descriptions were created and functional interconnections between posts were defined. More than half of the SMEs (52%) declared that they define job descriptions to some extent. In such cases employees are also responsible for executing other, emerging tasks. Around one out of four SMEs do not have defined tasks and responsibilities for employees – this means that employees fulfil ongoing activities.

In general, the investigated companies do not have a developed and formalised organisational structure. In 63.5% of cases, departments responsible for a particular scope of activities were created. One out of five companies (20%) have created departments and set cooperation and communication principles between them. Only 6% of SMEs claim that they have precisely defined hierarchical and

*Table 3.8* Relationships between employees

| | Share in % | | | | |
|---|---|---|---|---|---|
| | Completely disagree | Rather disagree | Rather agree | Completely agree | Hard to say |
| Employees interact solely on an occupational basis. | 12.5 | 26.5 | 36.5 | 24.5 | 0.0 |
| Employees create friendships with co-workers. | 7.5 | 18.0 | 49.0 | 22.5 | 3.0 |
| Employees create friendly relationships which are also maintained outside of the working environment. | 9.0 | 12.0 | 48.0 | 24.5 | 6.5 |
| Our employees make a team with strong relationships involving their families. | 7.5 | 10.5 | 51.0 | 24.5 | 6.5 |

functional relationships between job positions and departments. One out of every ten companies claims it has not yet undertaken any actions aimed at settling down and formalising organisational structure.

According to the gathered data, relationships in SMEs are based on both friendship and duties. One out of four companies (24.5%) claimed that its employees do not establish close, informal relationships, focusing only on cooperation while fulfilling tasks (see Table 3.8).

### *Internal Processes Complexity*

In order to evaluate the complexity of internal processes, respondents were asked to evaluate whether in their companies the processes listed in Table 3.9 are executed by themselves, partly supported by external partners, outsourced or not executed at all. Only 35.5% claimed they execute all the listed processes by themselves or with partial support from partners.

Within the most frequently run processes, only those directly referring to interactions with customers were highlighted: *customer relationship management* (54%) *and selling* (53%). However, *finance management* is the process run most frequently on their own (55.5%). It can be concluded that these processes are crucial in

*Table 3.9* Complexity of internal processes

| Process | Share in % | | | |
|---|---|---|---|---|
| | We execute it on our own | We execute it partly on our own | We outsource it | We do not run such a process |
| Finance management | 55.5 | 36.0 | 8.5 | 0.0 |
| Customer relationship management | 54.0 | 36.5 | 9.5 | 0.0 |
| Selling | 53.0 | 37.5 | 7.5 | 2.0 |
| Production/services planning | 49.5 | 33.0 | 13.5 | 4.0 |
| Purchase | 48.0 | 34.5 | 14.5 | 3.0 |
| Investment planning | 45.0 | 41.5 | 12.0 | 1.5 |
| Warehouse management | 44.5 | 33.5 | 13.5 | 8.5 |
| Accounting | 43.0 | 37.5 | 19.0 | 0.5 |
| Logistics | 43.0 | 38.0 | 11.5 | 7.5 |
| Payroll | 41.0 | 40.0 | 19.0 | 0.0 |
| Human resource management | 39.5 | 40.5 | 20.0 | 0.0 |
| Promotion and marketing | 38.5 | 46.0 | 14.0 | 1.5 |
| IT support | 33.5 | 42.0 | 22.5 | 2.0 |
| Research and development | 28.5 | 53.0 | 16.0 | 2.5 |

running a business and owners/managers want to have full control over their execution.

Interestingly, the most frequently outsourced processes were those requiring specialist knowledge. Around one out of every five companies claimed they use external providers in running processes that cover: IT (22.5%), human resource management (20%), payroll (19%) and accounting (19%). Additionally, around 40% of investigated SMEs confirmed they run only basic tasks related to these processes and use the support of external providers in more complex activities.

Among the companies that execute the processes listed in Table 3.8 fully or partly on their own, one out of every three declares it has defined and described them fully (see Table 3.10). Nearly half of the companies claim they have detailed procedures and schemes to run these processes. Thus, it can be concluded that around 75–88% of SMEs have introduced standards of how to run processes that are executed on their own. The exception refers to IT processes, which are described by procedures in as many as 70% of the companies.

*Table 3.10* The level of internal process formalisation

| Process | Share in % | | | |
|---|---|---|---|---|
| | We have detailed procedures | Most activities are included in procedures and schemes | Only some of the activities are included in procedures and schemes | We have no procedures referring to the process |
| Finance management | 33.3 | 54.6 | 9.8 | 2.2 |
| Warehouse management | 32.1 | 54.5 | 12.2 | 1.3 |
| Payroll | 38.3 | 48.2 | 11.1 | 2.5 |
| Accounting | 30.4 | 54.0 | 12.4 | 3.1 |
| Customer relations management | 34.3 | 49.7 | 12.2 | 3.9 |
| Human resource management | 30.0 | 53.1 | 16.3 | 0.6 |
| Production/services planning | 35.2 | 47.9 | 15.2 | 1.8 |
| Investments planning | 30.6 | 50.9 | 16.2 | 2.3 |
| Logistics | 30.9 | 49.4 | 17.9 | 1.9 |
| Purchase | 32.7 | 47.3 | 17.6 | 2.4 |
| Marketing and promotion | 30.2 | 49.1 | 17.2 | 3.6 |
| Research and development | 24.5 | 52.8 | 19.6 | 3.1 |
| Selling | 30.9 | 44.8 | 22.1 | 2.2 |
| IT support | 18.5 | 52.3 | 26.5 | 2.7 |

It should be stated that the process that directly corresponds with talent management – human resource management – is executed either fully or partly by 80% of the investigated SMEs. Use of external providers' support was claimed by 20% of companies and none of the investigated SMEs declared that they do not run HRM activities. Moreover, 30% of companies have introduced detailed HRM schemes and more than half (54%) claim they have included most HRM activities in internal procedures. Thus, it can be assumed that HRM is perceived as a process of high importance in SME management.

### Level of HR Professionalisation

Despite the fact that HRM procedures are fully developed in 30% of SMEs and 53% have introduced schemes concerning how to run particular activities, only 18.5% of the investigated companies declare that they have written down their HRM strategies. More than one in three (36%) have an HRM strategy (but not written down as a document), and 39% claim they have defined the main goals referring to most important HRM activities. On the one hand, this data confirms the importance of HRM in the investigated companies, but on the other hand, it shows that in SMEs, there is no strategic overview of HRM activities.

According to the respondents, personnel planning (87.5%) and employee acquisition (81%) are the issues most frequently addressed by organisational strategy. This may stem from the fact that providing the organisation with an appropriate quantity and quality of employees is a primary factor in assuring effective functioning. Three out of every four companies (73%) claim to include employee development and talent management issues in their organisational strategy.

Quotes in Box 3.2 illustrate how talent management is linked with the companies' strategies.

---

**BOX 3.2 LINK BETWEEN TM AND STRATEGY**

We have an organisational strategy that includes HR-related issues. We develop talents because we want them to create value for the company; we want to use their potential to assure the firm's development and common success. (Company H)

We have defined the main goals referring to the organisation's growth – talent management practices are developed in line with these goals. (Company E)

We define general goals for the next three to five years; these are the ideas we want to introduce. Additionally, we create detailed yearly plans and on their basis, we define ongoing operational goals. In our company, we meet weekly to define actions to be performed – talents play a crucial role in their execution. (Company I)

---

Despite the fact that the investigated companies link their HR activities with an organisational strategy and have internal procedures describing how these activities should be executed; HRM is not designed as a complex system. On the basis of the gathered data, it can be concluded that HRM in the investigated SMEs is impoverished and concentrates mainly on employee acquisition (see Table 3.11). Of the investigated SMEs, 53% claim to execute

*Table 3.11* Scope of HRM activities in the investigated SMEs

|                                                  | Share in % |
|--------------------------------------------------|------------|
| Long-term staffing plans                         | 42.5       |
| Recruitment and selection                        | 53.0       |
| Adaptation of newly hired employees              | 52.5       |
| Competence development planning                  | 42.5       |
| Competence development execution                 | 31.0       |
| Employee appraisals                              | 29.0       |
| Job valuation                                    | 31.0       |
| Managing remuneration system                     | 24.0       |
| Employee satisfaction                            | 16.0       |
| Job rotation and internal transfer programmes    | 10.5       |

*Note*: Respondents could choose any applicable.

recruitment and selection process, and 52.5% to run adaptation of newly hired workers. Additionally, 42.5% of the interviewed SMEs take a long-term perspective with regarding to staff planning and prepare competence development plans. It can be concluded that all the above-mentioned activities are aimed at providing SMEs with an appropriate (and expected) level of employees' knowledge, skills and abilities. This can be achieved by both employee acquisition and employee development.

The investigated companies pay less attention to activities aimed at performance and engagement improvement. Only 29% execute appraisals, 24% manage their remuneration system and 16% conduct employee satisfaction surveys.

On the basis of the gathered data, it can be concluded that the level of human resource management professionalisation in the investigated SMEs is rather low. Despite the fact that respondents link HRM activities with organisation strategy, most companies focus solely on employee acquisition. Other HRM processes are executed in only a few companies and in an informal way. The lack of HRM subject-specific knowledge can be the main reason for establishing cooperation with external partners.

## Analysis of Contextual Factors

Due to the heterogeneity of the sample (with regard to the sector, size and range), an in-depth analysis did not allow the identification of factors that would coherently describe the context of SMEs' functioning. However, on the basis of respondents' answers, it was possible to recognise the specificity of contextual factors. This was achieved by taking into account the most frequently selected answers.

*Table 3.12* General characteristics of external factors

| Factor | Characteristics |
| --- | --- |
| Employee availability | Problems with hiring employees in specialist positions (57%) |
| Requirements regarding specific competences | Limited, only occasionally are some requirements towards specific competences defined (50.5%) |
| Industry specificity | Niche sector – well-grounded (46%) or emerging (3.5%) |
| Key factors impacting the potential for growth in the given industry | Experience (53.5%), price (47.5%), brand (41%) |
| SME image on the labour market | SMEs are perceived as companies that: create friendly working environment (36.5%), offer jobs adjusted to employees' competences (33.5%), offer attractive working conditions (32.5%) |
| Competition | Moderate, 40% declared that they have more than ten competitors (50% in case of SMEs operating on domestic market); international companies are the main competitors |

With regard to external factors (see Table 3.12), the most important seems to be the labour market situation. Most of the investigated companies (57%) face problems with hiring employees in specialist positions. Additionally, half of the companies (50.5%) claim they define some specific requirements concerning employee competences. In their opinion, processes that require unique competences are only occasionally executed, and specific knowledge, skills and abilities do not narrow down the number of potential candidates. In these companies, the expected performance can be achieved by using general competences that are also applicable in other companies, even those operating in very different industries.

Only one out of every three SMEs operates in a well-grounded standard industry, but nearly half of the companies (49.5%), operate in well-established or emerging niche sectors. In such industries, in which there are limited numbers of potential clients, building relationships with customers as well as focusing on quality and innovativeness may determine a competitive advantage. This may result in the greater importance of human capital.

Of the factors impacting SMEs' growth and development potential, the following were most frequently highlighted: experience (53%), price (47.5%) and brand (41%). It can be concluded that among the investigated companies, know-how (which constitutes experience and image) is very important. However, these companies have to pay greater attention to the costs of running a business so that their prices correspond with the market level.

The provided data shows that SMEs create a friendly working environment and offer attractive working conditions and interesting jobs that are adjusted to the employees' expectations. In the respondents' opinions, these attributes create a positive image of SMEs on the labour market.

The investigated SMEs operate on markets with moderate competition. Around 40–45% of companies operating on local, regional and international markets and 50% of those operating on domestic market, declare they have more than ten competitors. Interestingly, companies operating on regional, domestic and international markets face the highest competition from international companies. They declare less competition from companies operating on the same markets.

One of the internal factors (see Table 3.13) that shape the context of SME functioning are sources of competitive advantage. According to the gathered data, those relating to the way in which SMEs

*Table 3.13* General characteristics of internal factors

| Factor | Characteristics |
| --- | --- |
| Sources of competitive advantage | Innovativeness (83.5%), time to react on changes (80%) |
| Decision-making process | Highly centralised; in 74.5% of cases, the owner/manager makes decisions and sets goals on their own |
| Job structuring | Low; only 23% have developed and introduced job descriptions including tasks and duties |
| Structuring functional and hierarchical interdependencies | Very low; only 6% have a defined organisational structure of interdependencies between job positions and departments |
| Employee relationships | Friendly and informal; in 75.5% of cases, employees constitute a well-performing team and maintain their relationships even outside of the work environment |
| Internal process complexity | Low; only 35.5% of SMEs execute all internal processes fully or partly on their own |
| Processes formalisation | Moderate; one out of every three investigated companies have developed internal procedures in detail; half of the companies developed schemes referring to most activities and tasks in particular processes |
| HRM professionalisation | Low; only 18.5% have an HRM strategy in a written form; none of the investigated companies execute all listed HR processes; some of the processes are introduced only in a narrow group of companies |

react to market changes seem most significant. Respondents most frequently indicated innovativeness (83.5%) and the time of reacting to changes.

Taking into account the management system as a contextual factor, it can be stated that the decision-making process in SMEs is highly centralised. In 74.5% of companies, decisions are made by owners/managers (in 22.5% of cases, owners/managers make decisions on their own; in 52% of cases, employees may influence them to a small extent). Tasks and duties are not defined in most of the investigated SMEs. Nearly one out of four companies (23%) claim that they prepare job descriptions. This may result in a very low level of organisational structure formalisation, as only 6% declared that they set and specify functional and hierarchical interdependencies between posts and departments. In one out of every ten companies, these interdependencies were not defined and described at all. In the remaining organisations, only basic relationships between departments were settled. In the respondents' opinion, in most investigated companies, employees constitute a well-performing team that maintains friendly relationships even outside of the work environment.

Most of the investigated SMEs do not execute all processes related to organisational functioning on their own. They either use external partners' support or outsource them. Of the processes that are most frequently introduced and run by organisations on their own are those related to finance management and relationships with customers. Additionally, processes requiring subject-specific knowledge (accounting, payroll, human resource management, IT, marketing and promotion) are in most cases either executed with professional support or outsourced. Such a situation may stem from the focus on primary activities (most important, crucial) and processes in investigated companies. Of the SMEs which execute processes on their own or use external support, only one in every three has developed and introduced internal procedures. Half of them have schemes referring to only some of the most important activities. A low level of internal process formalisation refers also to human resource management. Only 18.5% of companies have written down an HRM strategy. More than one out of every three companies (36%) declares that it has developed an HRM strategy but not in the form of an internal document. The main HRM goals and activities concern planning for new staff (87.5%) and acquisition of personnel (81%). HRM-related activities do not constitute a complex system, as only 29% conduct employee appraisals, 24%

manage their remuneration system and 16% undertake employee satisfaction surveys.

The conducted analyses confirmed that the investigated SMEs operate in various contexts. This supports the conclusions drawn by Thunnissen et al. (2013), Gallardo-Gallardo et al. (2019) and Thunnissen and Gallardo-Gallardo (2019) that contextual factors may have an impact upon talent management practices, especially when SMEs apply the 'best-fit' approach. However, it can be stated that the nature of external factors in SMEs is, in some regards, similar to that found in large organisations. All companies suffer from a lack of specialists – for many of them, experience, brand and price play a crucial role in building a competitive advantage, and these companies face high market competition. Nonetheless, the distinctiveness can be identified when taking into account internal factors. The shape of organisation-specific contextual factors makes it possible to conclude that SMEs significantly differ from large organisations. For example, the decisions are made mostly by the owner – there are no organisational structures developed and the complexity of internal processes is low as SMEs do not execute many HR processes and they do not have an HR strategy developed. This leads to the conclusion expressed by Gallardo-Gallardo et al. (2019) that research results on talent management obtained from investigating large or multinational corporations do not reflect the situation with SMEs.

# 4 Talent Management Practices in the Surveyed Companies

In the literature on the topic of talent management, it is emphasised that talent management practices are determined by numerous factors, including the understanding of talent by managers and owners and the importance ascribed to it in the functioning of a company (Pocztowski & Pauli, 2013). The level of human resource management professionalisation and contextual factors are of great significance here as they influence the implementation of unique solutions in terms of talent management (Gallardo-Gallardo et al., 2017; Krishnan & Scullion, 2017). Additionally, cultural factors in a given country play an important role (Skuza et al., 2013; Valverde at al., 2013; Festing et al., 2017) along with the situation on the labour market and the stage of development of a company (Krishnan & Scullion, 2017). Taking into consideration the diversity of approaches to human resource management in SMEs, one should assume that talent management practices in such companies can be also implemented in a different way than in large organisations (Pauli, 2018). Even though the range of such practices may be similar to that of large organisations, the method of their implementation may be different. Moreover, it should be noted that SMEs do not constitute a homogenous category. Considering the number of employees, which has a significant impact on the architecture of the human resources and talent management systems, we may find among them micro, small and medium-sized companies. The diversity of approaches to talent management in such companies stems from a few factors. Furthermore, the question of the above-mentioned diversity raised in the existing literature on the subject is also reflected in the results of the research presented below.

## Understanding of Talent in the Surveyed Companies

The literature proves the importance of talented employees for organisations; however, it provides evidence that results rather from a theoretical discourse than from rational and practical actions.

This also applies in the field of challenges addressed to HR specialists. Indeed, the problem seems to be crucial, especially for small companies. Talented employees are demanding and at the same time, they promise more than employees who are not talents. They demand much more with regard to investments (financial, personal etc.) than others. The HR department has to apply a specific knowledge to them. Unfortunately, in small organisations, where professionalism of the personnel function is scarce, it is not enough to retain talents. While talents are recognised as being valuable assets and useful for achieving organisational goals, deficiencies exist with regard to precisely identifying the specifics of talents' skills and abilities. Nevertheless, the popularity of talent management concept is growing and practical solutions are clearly situational and contextual. The context here is the size of an organisation, the knowledge of talent, the level of professionalism in performing the personal function which results in the diversity of available solutions, financial issues and the market position of the given company. The context also includes extra-organisational factors, which are, however, beyond the influence of companies.

The results of empirical studies on talented employees that can be found in the existing literature make it possible to assume that SMEs focus on finding employees who, in the reality of a small organisation, would be able to adopt various roles and perform many different tasks. This has been confirmed by studies by Heneman, Tansky and Camp (2000) and Festing et al. (2013). Such a theory is contrary to what is usually associated with 'talent', namely uniqueness and clear specialisation, which was mentioned in Chapter 1. Furthermore, a wide range of employees' competences in a company are closely related to their development and experience, which emphasises the importance of what is learned, experienced and shaped. Thus, it confirms the manner of understanding talent as an acquired skill, not as a kind of gift.

SMEs are important entities where talent can be developed. They create more opportunities for individuals to get to know their strengths and weaknesses as well as interests. Research conducted by Storey, Saridakis, Sen-Gupta, Edwards and Blackburn (2010) proved that SMEs enable individuals to become more focused on their tasks due to the reduced level of bureaucracy and formalisation. Additionally, innovations introduced in such companies are more significant than in large organisations (Dundon & Wilkinson, 2009).

When we consider the arguments for and against addressing the issue of talents in SMEs, it should be clearly indicated that the influence of talented employees' work output on the situation of a company is much greater than in large organisations (Festing et al., 2013). This seems to be a sufficient justification for transferring knowledge in this field to HR positions in such companies. This conclusion is reinforced by research conducted in Polish companies from the SME sector. The research showed that in such companies, talented employees were regarded as people who were particularly important for their functioning.

This was clearly illustrated by a large proportion of positive responses from 88% of the surveyed people (answers 'yes' – 42.5%, and 'rather yes' – 45.5% were included). Only 2% of respondents did not confirm the importance of this group of employees. Added together, the answers 'no' and 'rather no' accounted for 10.5%. The data is presented in Table 4.1.

Commenting on the results shown above, one may conclude that the issue of talents is recognised and considered to be significant in Polish companies. However, the question arises as to what is talent in these organisations. Defining the referent would enable the identification of appropriate instruments for its management. Thus, the next step in the research was to identify the semantic scope of the term 'talent' and compare it with the existing definitional suggestions.

The results of previous research conducted in 2007 by a team of researchers from Cracow University of Economics as well as the analysis of numerous publications in terms of both their theoretical and empirical spheres enabled the selection of the most popular and frequently used expressions. It is worth noting that they were of clearly organisational origin and concern organisational management. Other explanations – related to the psychology of creativity, education or other disciplines – did not appear at all or represented a tiny proportion, thus they were not included in the research.

*Table 4.1* Importance of talents in investigated SMEs

| *In your company, is great importance attached to talented employees?* | *Share (in %)* |
| --- | --- |
| Yes | 42.50 |
| Rather yes | 45.50 |
| Rather no | 8.50 |
| No | 2.00 |
| Hard to say | 1.50 |

The research proved that in Polish SMEs, 'talent' was most frequently understood as *an employee with exceptional/outstanding abilities*. This was confirmed by a largest share of respondents in our research (38%). The interpretation of this result shows that a talent is a person with acquired abilities to perform specific tasks, so it is a person who has learned to be proficient and who brings this proficiency to a company or develops it in the organisation.

Such an understanding of talent refers to the definitions by Silzer and Dowell (2010) and Cheese et al., (2008). This approach can be described as being objective, close to inclusive and seeing talent in the background of a position and, to a lesser extent, a person. The essential characteristic of talent understood in such a way is its acquisition/learning during one's work for an organisation. Table 4.2 contains a summary of the answers received.

Slightly fewer (36.5%) respondents described 'talent' as *a person with a high level of performance*. An efficiency connotation is clearly visible here, which means that an organisation used work results as a criterion for identifying talents. Such an interpretation of talent corresponds to Jerico's (2001) definition and puts greater emphasis on the work output (not the contribution to an organisation). In an organisation, an employee 'becomes' a talent as a result of his or her high level of performance. The value of talented employees for a company is variable; talent is regarded as learned and has the possibility of being developed as well as related to a position.

At only one percentage point lower, 35% of the respondents referred to 'a talented employee' as *a knowledge-intensive worker* – a knowledgeable person. Thus, it seems that talent includes, in part,

*Table 4.2* The notion of talent in investigated companies

|  | *Share in %* |
| --- | --- |
| A person with a high level of performance/a highly efficient person | 36.50 |
| A person with extensive knowledge – 'a knowledge-intensive worker' | 35.50 |
| A person with exceptional talents/interests | 30.50 |
| A person with exceptional skills | 38.00 |
| A person who has a great influence on others | 25.00 |
| A highly qualified employee/a professional | 32.00 |
| A very experienced employee | 18.00 |
| A creative person who introduces various innovations and solutions | 17.00 |
| A person who is actively involved in the implementation of various projects and tasks | 14.50 |

making a contribution to an organisation in the form of individual learning aptitude and personal motivation and, in part, contributing to an environment that creates such opportunities. Talent here can be described as being acquired and having the possibility to be developed, exclusive, related to an individual, and to a lesser extent, involving a position with a large dose of universality.

The next approach to talent in Polish SMEs stresses professionalism and expertise as criteria for distinguishing talented employees (*it is a highly qualified employee/a professional*). Such an understanding was indicated by 32% of the respondents. People considered to be talented are those with extensive knowledge and experience in certain specific fields that are significant for an organisation. The essence of talent understood in such a way is experience acquired with time and related to particular organisational conditions. Thus, knowledge and practice are necessary as they lead to a high level of professionalism. Talent can be described as being acquired, developed and inclusive, related to a position and situational.

Talent as *a person with exceptional gifts or/and interests* was indicated by 30.5% of respondents. This way of understanding emphasises talent as an endowment – a gift bestowed on an organisation (thus, recognised when entering a company). Talent here is a distinctive feature of an individual, it is unique (exclusive), strongly universal and possible to be developed in specific conditions created by a company.

The next definition of 'talent' present in Polish SMEs is *a person who has a great influence on others*. This was indicated by 25% of the people surveyed. Such an understanding of talent is mostly linked with leadership in an organisation and managerial positions. It is derived from one of the trends in talent management where talent is in fact leadership talent (Sheehan, 2012; Björkman & Mäkëla, 2013). In this approach, it is universalistic and exclusive, related to an individual and, being a gift, resistant to development.

The participants of the survey also regarded 'talent' as *a very experienced employee* (18%). This means that talent is an acquired competence. Its advantage is related to the fact that it can be shaped in an organisation in accordance with its needs. As it is associated with an organisation, it is situational and relating to a position rather than to a person. Such an interpretation of talent means that the number of talents is constantly updated due to the inclusion of employees who gain their experience. It is possible to find here references to definitions by Cheese et al. (2008) and Williams (2000).

Slightly less frequently (17%), respondents mentioned that they understood 'talent' as creativity (*a creative person who introduces various innovations and solutions*). Talent here is seen in the framework of an exceptionally developed feature, the value of which results from innovative solutions and their importance for the implementation of the company's objectives. This corresponds with a definition by Bethke-Langenegger et al. (2011). Talent interpreted in such a way can be described as a gift brought to a company, distinctive for an individual, exclusive and universalistic. It can be developed to a very small extent.

The quotes in Box 4.1 illustrate variants of defining talents in Polish SMEs.

---

**BOX 4.1 DIFFERENT EXPLANATIONS OF TALENT IN INVESTIGATED SMES**

For me and our organisation, a talent is a person who is distinguished by his or her attitude and commitment to the life of the company, who wants to develop in a more than average way in a given subject and aims to do so. They are not limited only to their paper, so to speak, responsibilities, that is, their designated duties, but they also get willingly involved in the life of the company. They are also eager to look for development paths for themselves. (...) They do not wait for our offers; they take the initiative themselves. Such a person is more self-conscious than other people. And this self-awareness is also translated into the company. (Company E)

Talent is such a skill of candidates that allows them to stand out and be specialists, above other employees. This skill allows them to be themselves (...), which is consistent with their passions. Their talent improves their functioning in the company and is an added value for the company (Company A)

First of all, talent is a skill that allows a person to be extremely good at something; a skill that makes him or her stand out. (Company G)

By talent we often mean that someone can paint or sing very well. But it's not just that. There is also a talent, for instance, to win people over or to be able to solve problems. To see a nice solution in situations where others cannot see it. (Company D)

Talent is an ability to do many things at the same time (...) and not to fail in any of them. It is the ability to do several or a dozen or so things (simultaneously). (Company I)

A certain property of a person, a certain trait, a predisposition to be particularly good at something. (Company O)

---

Less frequently (14.5%), respondents chose the answer *a person who is actively involved in the implementation of various projects and tasks.* Such an approach emphasises a wide range of employees' skills rather than special, outstanding qualities. This means that talent here is situational, referred to as acquired and possible to be developed. The emphasis here is placed on the employees' contribution, not on their results. It can be described as inclusive and related to a position. In an extreme form of this approach '... *in some cases, "the talent" might refer to the entire employee population*' as suggested by Silzer and Dowell (2010, p. 14).

Table 4.3 presents the characteristic features of various indicators of talent, which can be used to create a specific model of the perception of talent in Polish SMEs. Its most significant characteristics are identifying talent at the selection process and talent being susceptible to development. Almost to the same extent, the source of talent is perceived as being acquired rather than innate. It is linked to a person, is situational and inclusive.

When the principles from the above model are translated into organisational practice, it means that a company can seek people with particular skills/features/experience, which are identified during the recruitment process (identification). The choice of a candidate with the desired characteristics will result in their inclusion into the pool of talents (inclusiveness), which means that the group of people considered to be talents is large. A talented worker can be subject to development activities (susceptibility to development) taken up by a company due to its present or future needs (situational). In the interpretation of a small Polish company, talent is acquired and linked to a person, not to a function performed or a position held. This means that talent in an organisation can be built with the use of available instruments and shaped in accordance with its needs.

The statements in Box 4.2 provide indications of the features of talent in Polish SMEs.

Does such an interpretation of the term 'a talented worker' differ significantly from 'a worker who is not a talent'? It seems that the differences, if they appear, are minor. A clear tendency in companies not to firmly stress the uniqueness of talent results from the fact that employees are selected carefully, which in turn results in a small margin of error in the case of a wrong choice in a situation in which certain investments were made in an employed person. The financial consequences of a recruitment failure are particularly burdensome for small companies and another recruitment process makes them even greater. Thus, there is a

Table 4.3 A summary of the characteristics of talent referring to particular indicators

| Designatum: / Characteristics: | Given | Acquired | Inclusive | Exclusive | Universal | Situational | Position | Person | Entry | Exit | Developed | Constant |
|---|---|---|---|---|---|---|---|---|---|---|---|---|
| A person with a high level of performance/a highly efficient person | | + | + | | + | | | + | | + | + | |
| A person with extensive knowledge – 'a knowledge-intensive worker' | | + | | + | | + | | + | + | | + | |
| A person with exceptional talents/interests | + | | | + | | + | | + | + | | + | |
| A person with exceptional skills | | + | + | | | + | | + | + | | + | |
| A person who has a great influence on others | + | | | + | + | | | + | + | | | + |
| A highly qualified employee/a professional | | + | + | | + | | + | | + | | + | |
| A very experienced employee | | + | + | | + | | + | | + | | + | |
| A creative person who introduces various innovations and solutions | + | | | + | | + | + | | | + | | + |
| A person who is actively involved in the implementation of various projects and tasks | | + | + | | | + | + | | + | | + | |
| Total: | 3 | 6 | 5 | 4 | 4 | 5 | 4 | 5 | 7 | 2 | 7 | 2 |

---

**BOX 4.2 FEATURES OF TALENT IN POLISH SMES**

If we see someone with exceptional skills, we try to expand them somehow and help to develop them. (Company M)

This is undoubtedly a kind of gift, it is something, you can say, that appears by itself. Something that is in a person. It can relate to any area. (Company D)

---

tendency to find a versatile candidate who will be able to perform various activities rather than a person with exceptional skills and specific requirements who does not guarantee a desired result. Thus, a talented person in Polish SMEs is not a 'gifted' person who brings his or her passion to an organisation and produces exceptional results that improve the situation of a company. Although undoubtedly, a small company is the perfect place for the development of individual passions if they correspond to its organisational objectives.

The above-mentioned respondents were people responsible for HR activities in their companies. Thus, their knowledge on the issue in question was frequently closely connected with their everyday experiences on an informal basis. Also, their activities in an organisation were not fully or even partly formalised. However, in order to shape the pool of talents and manage it properly, it is necessary to transfer knowledge to all entities of an organisation, regardless of whether they are entities affected by the activities or those affecting others (Pauli, 2020). Consequently, an attempt was made to recognise such organisational practices that are aimed at promoting or transferring knowledge on the policy of an organisation towards talented employees. For details see Table 4.4.

*Table 4.4* Awareness of meaning of talent in surveyed organisations

|  | *Share in %* |
| --- | --- |
| The interpretation of the term 'talent' is defined in our company and communicated to all employees. | 27.50 |
| Meaning of talent is communicated to people on managerial positions/superior positions. | 40.50 |
| Everyone knows what talent is; there is no need to explain that. | 20.00 |
| There is no single definition of talent in our organisation. | 12.00 |

The research proved that most frequently (40.5% of respondents), knowledge of understanding the term 'a talented worker' is communicated to employees in managerial positions. Such prerogatives provide the biggest chances to identify such an employee and, with the use of appropriate instruments, retain and to develop his or her talent in a company. Of the surveyed companies, 27.5% have, according to respondents, a clearly defined interpretation of talent transferred to all employees. This is surely the most desirable situation when all the interested workers are able to participate in the programme designed for talents. Thus, it is not an arbitrary definition of the management but a decision on the part of an employee to take inclusive actions.

In 20% of the surveyed companies, it is assumed that everyone knows what 'talent' refers to, so there are not any measures taken in order to spread the knowledge. Such an approach results in competence ambiguity regarding the tasks of the managing entities as well as the confusion of employees who have subjective/informal knowledge on the issue.

The last group of answers (12%) pointed to the lack of one existing definition of talent in an organisation. This means that these companies do not consider the issue of talent to be significant and do not take any measures aimed at identifying such people. After combining the answers with the previous ones ('everyone knows what talent is; there is no need to explain that'), it becomes apparent that the issue of talents in almost one-third of Polish SMEs (32%) is not addressed. Consequently, any activities related to it are occasional. They are usually of an informal nature and they do not depend on the condition and the market position of a company.

The analysis of answers received in the context of the question about the importance attached to talented people in organisations proves the existence of a certain convergence: 10.5% of responses show that the issue of talent is not significant for an organisation and 12% of responses indicate that there is no clear definition of this term provided by an organisation. One may assume that those two results are mutually verified.

The results of qualitative research show that the concept of talent is specified and/or formalised in Polish companies to varying degrees. This is illustrated by the following statements (see Box 4.3).

---

**BOX 4.3 THE LEVEL OF TALENT MEANING FORMALISATION**

In fact, there are no such guidelines. Managers assess their subordinates on their own and determine whether their level of development is better than in the case of others. There is no single definition, or no policy written down. (Company O)

We have a book on talent management. Well yes, in the foundations of the company, an employee who can be referred to as a talent is a person who in a special way influences the growth of the company's value and has above-average potential for further development and proves his or her worth on senior managerial positions. We have developed such a definition. (Company P)

They are people with above-average abilities and skills, standing out in a team. In our company, talent is understood in such a way, although no one makes it clear. (Company R)

We examine the team we have. There are interim evaluations, conversations with employees to identify who is a talent. Based on the analysis of the team, we identify and develop talents. (Company H)

---

To sum up the considerations on the issue of talent and its practical operationalisation in small and medium-sized Polish companies, the following conclusions can be drawn:

- In over 10% of companies from this sector, little attention is attached to the issue of talented workers; over 80% of them expressed interest in this issue.
- The understanding of talent is mostly combined with exceptional skills, high efficiency and knowledge. Thus, talent is considered an acquired disposition, is situational and has the possibility to be developed. It is not linked to passion which in the long run would enable the generation of results of great significance for an organisation. In this sense, a talented employee varies only slightly from an employee who is not a talent and definitely does not require expensive or special management instruments.

- The recognition of the issue of talent in the surveyed organisations is at a relatively low level: in about 30% of them, the
  designatum of the term is not clearly defined and it is not iden-
  tifiable by all members of an organisation. This fact prevents an
  individual from deciding about their own path of professional
  development.

## Talent's Roles and Competences

When considering talent management practices in the broader internal and external context of the functioning of a company as well
as with respect to the effects of its operation, the tasks and roles
that talented employees are entrusted with seem a significant issue. These are crucial for the possibilities of taking advantage of
talents in the implementation of business processes. The roles and
tasks of talented employees are related to competences necessary
for their efficient implementation. These issues were also part of the
research, the results of which are presented in Table 4.5.

As can be seen in the Table 4.5, talented employees most frequently perform tasks related to their qualifications and to the requirements of their positions. They occasionally take up other, more
specialised tasks associated with coordination and control (37% of
responses). Moreover, the character of talented employees' work is

*Table 4.5* The nature of tasks executed by talented employees

|  | Share in % |
| --- | --- |
| Only tasks that concern their qualifications/skills related to their job positions | 14.50 |
| Mainly tasks that concern their qualifications related to their job positions, yet occasionally also other, specialised tasks (e.g. coordination, control) | 37.00 |
| Usually specialised tasks/functions, e.g. sales, logistics, finances, or/and tasks related to the management of specialised processes, such as innovation, building the image of a brand, promotion | 32.50 |
| Management tasks that enable them to widely use their potential | 9.50 |
| The tasks and roles of mentoring other employees and advisers of people in managerial positions | 3.00 |
| Talented employees do not have strictly assigned tasks and roles; they take on tasks and roles which result from the current conditions | 3.50 |

described with the use of specialised tasks and functions performed in various areas of the companies' activities or related to the management of specialised processes (32.5%). The above-mentioned facts prove that the scope of tasks conducted by talented employees in the surveyed companies is to the largest extent connected both with the use of their qualifications for their positions and with fulfilling specialised functions. Much less frequently, talented workers exclusively perform tasks related to their positions (14.5%) or perform managerial functions (9.5%) and very rarely, they do not have clearly defined tasks or they perform the roles of mentors for other employees or advisers of managers.

The statements in Box 4.4 are an additional illustration of the scope of tasks performed by talented employees.

---

**BOX 4.4 THE SCOPE OF TASKS PERFORMED BY TALENTS**

In the group of our talents, the vast majority have ambitions and a willingness to manage and lead a team. They coordinate the work of others, plan their work and account for what happens. Also, we have in this group people who directly signal that they are interested in a specialist career, that they find themselves in their field and want to specialise in it even more. These people more often develop their own services, come up with ideas interesting for the market and clients and independently develop such projects. (Company E)

Talented employees are involved in task and project teams. We use such a concept here. Mostly they are new projects or implementations of new innovative solutions for us or our clients. Talents play a significant role in them; they are experts or they manage projects and simply develop certain projects and then implement them. (Company P)

We have several people from the pool of talents who are project managers. However, it is not a rule that each talented employee must be a project manager. Some are programmers, but they are not communicative, and they do not like to contact clients or team members. We use them by entrusting them with the implementation of specific projects that interest them and where they can exploit their potential. (Company F)

*(Continued)*

---

Talents have more freedom of action. They get a specific list of tasks. They have the right to make corrections, conclusions in the team or present their preferences. (Company H)

Employees who are talented and trusted by the boss are people who, if they are assigned a task, will do everything in their power to do it. It is a matter of a sense of responsibility for work. (Company I)

Talented employees talk more, and contacts with them are more frequent. They talk not only about current issues but also about the future of the company, about emerging problems. (Company Q).

Tasks and organisational roles performed by talented workers are strictly connected with their competences. One of the issues that the research focused on was to recognise the importance of various competences of talents in the surveyed companies. The results obtained in the research are given in Table 4.6.

The figures in Table 4.6 show that the greatest significance in the surveyed companies is attached to specialist knowledge related mostly to the work stream of talented employees. In 40.5% of the companies in question, this competence area was regarded as key and in 46% as important. This competence area was clearly recognised as crucial in comparison with other competences among which relationship building and cooperation skills are treated as key and important competences (73.5% and 73%, respectively). Moreover, our attention should be drawn to the fact that all the competence areas of talented workers that were mentioned in the table were regarded at least as useful. Only occasionally were they referred to as minor or irrelevant. It is worth emphasising here that there is a great deal of importance attached to the issue of competence concerning efficiency, which includes goal and result orientation, determination to achieve goals and the ability to deal with difficult situations. The results of the research presented in Table 4.6 indicate that it is regarded as a key competence by 24% of the surveyed companies, as an important competence by 42.5% and as a useful competence by 31%.

The statements listed in Box 4.5 illustrate the importance of various competences as well as other features of talented people.

*Table 4.6* The significance of competences of talented employees

| Competence areas | The significance of competences (share in %) | | | | |
|---|---|---|---|---|---|
| | Key | Important | Useful | Minor | Irrelevant |
| Subject-specific knowledge related to the main work stream of a talented employee | 40.50 | 46.00 | 12.50 | 1.00 | 0.00 |
| Business knowledge concerning the sector or the market on which a company operates | 27.00 | 41.50 | 30.50 | 0.50 | 0.50 |
| Language skills | 21.00 | 40.00 | 33.00 | 5.50 | 0.50 |
| Communication skills (communicating, presenting materials, public speaking) | 21.00 | 38.00 | 31.00 | 9.50 | 0.50 |
| Relationship-building skills (making contacts, building and maintaining contacts, customer orientation and networking) | 26.00 | 47.00 | 21.50 | 5.50 | 0.00 |
| Cooperation (cooperation skills, coordinating tasks and organising other people's work) | 29.50 | 44.00 | 23.50 | 3.00 | 0.00 |
| Planning skills (time management, planning activities, creating schedules, establishing priorities, defining objectives and long-term thinking) | 23.00 | 46.50 | 27.00 | 3.50 | 0.00 |
| Competences related to effectiveness (goal and result orientation, determination, dealing with difficult situations) | 24.00 | 42.50 | 31.00 | 2.50 | 0.00 |

---

**BOX 4.5  THE IMPORTANCE OF PARTICULAR TALENT'S COMPETENCES**

According to our competence model, we have several key competences, which include analytical skills, communication, knowledge of English and goal orientation (Company P)

Depending on the project, we need people who would have contact with clients and be open in addition to having strictly technical skills. (Company F)

We place great emphasis on employees' values. Not necessarily on their experience, only on values. From the beginning of the company's operation, we have been looking for people who have specific personality traits. (Company A)

In general, the construction is that we work together. So, teamwork. We require independence, creativity and decision making from employees – of course, these decisions are consulted with the director or with me. It's about combining strong personalities who can find themselves in difficult, often international projects, but teamwork is also advisable. (Company K)

Each department has different requirements. In the case of an upholsterer, experience counts, but so does speed combined with accuracy. In the case of a salesman, communication skills, the organisation of work and honesty are important, because this is someone who we let out. For people managing production activities, the desirable characteristics include discipline, communication and planning skills as well as a sense of organising certain things. (Company D)

The attributes that we seek in candidates are a desire to develop, commitment and interest in a given topic. (Company B)

We regard people as talents when they have potential in which we want to invest. I ask myself a question about who I would take with me if I changed my job. The main features of talents are openness and the acceptance of changes, because I like changes. (Company Q)

---

The link between the character of talented employees' work and the significance attached to particular competence areas is an interesting cognitive aspect. In the surveyed companies, where the task and roles of talented employees are most frequently seen in the framework of the requirements of their jobs, occasionally complemented by other specialist tasks, the greatest importance was attached to specialist knowledge related to performed tasks. This was referred to as a key competence by 41.89% of the companies in question and as an important competence by 50% of them. This competence area was also rated highly among companies, which defined the character of talented employees' work as performing specialist tasks and managing specialist processes. In our survey, 44.62% of the companies regarded the significance of specialist knowledge as key and 43.08% considered them important. The greatest significance, however, was attached to this competence in those companies in which the work stream of talented employees was described as performing managerial tasks, which enabled exploitation of the considerable potential of this group of workers. This competence was regarded as key by 47.37% of the surveyed companies and the same percentage described it as important. Additionally, in this group the importance of business knowledge of the market and the sector in which the company operates was also evaluated at a very high level. It was considered to be a key competence by 42.11% and an important competence by 47.37% of the respondents. Shaping social relations and cooperation and coordinating and organising tasks were the highest rated important competences as evident in 68.42% and 63.16% of the responses, respectively.

For comparison, it can be mentioned here that in the group of companies where talent was seen solely in terms of tasks attached to particular work positions, there was a lower percentage of respondents for whom competences presented in Table 4.6 were key. For example, the area of specialist knowledge as a key competence received 24.14% of the responses, business knowledge received 17.24% and the other competences received between 10.34% and 13.79%. Cooperation skills, coordinating and organising tasks (55.17%) and the ability to shape social relations (48.28%) were indicated most frequently as significant competence areas.

While analysing talent management in SMEs in terms of its impact on the effects of the companies' operation, one should mention the data on the importance of the issue of competence are related directly to efficiency. The largest percentage of responses that it was a key competence was recorded in the group of companies that defined the nature of talented employees' work as mostly performing tasks attached to particular positions and occasionally specialised tasks. It accounted for 40.54% of the responses and it significantly exceeded the corresponding responses in the other groups of companies. Competences related to efficiency were regarded as important to the largest degree in the group of companies that described the character of talented employees' work as performing managerial tasks, which enabled them to use their high potential. Such responses were observed in 52.63% of the companies. Then, there were companies which defined the character of talented employees' work as performing specialised functions and managing specialised processes (49.23%).

The above-mentioned data proves that the character of talented employees' work, defined by the nature of tasks, functions and roles in an organisation, is a factor determining the importance attached to particular competency domains in SMEs.

## Overview of Talent Management Practices in the Investigated Companies

In general, talent management is a sequence of activities aimed at identifying, recruiting, developing and retaining talents. The majority of definitions that appear in the literature on the subject include the above elements, irrespective of various approaches to the understanding of the term 'talent', to talent management or the lack of an existing definition. In other words, the above-mentioned processes are the very essence of talent management, taking the form of specific, more or less formalised configurations in particular organisations. Actions taken within their framework can also be included in the processes of human resources management as they can be addressed to certain selected groups of employees considered to be talented.

Results of research on talent management practices in the surveyed SMEs are presented below. As pointed out earlier, talent management processes in SMEs may be similar to those implemented in large companies; however, it may be expected that particular solutions will be varied due to their specific character, the internal differentiation of this group, their operating context as well as other factors described in Chapter 3. Table 4.7 presents data illustrating tasks implemented within the framework of talent management in the companies in question.

As can be seen in Table 4.7, the scope of activities undertaken within the framework of talent management is broad and it includes most of the tasks that are the subject of human resources management. The enterprises surveyed were the most active in the area of identifying talents inside organisations (45.5%), recruiting and selecting (40%) as well as developing and training talented employees (41.50%).

*Table 4.7* The scope of tasks within the framework of talent management

|  | Share in % |
| --- | --- |
| Seeking talents outside an organisation | 20.00 |
| Identifying talents inside an organisation | 45.50 |
| Recruiting and selecting talents | 40.00 |
| Developing and training talents | 41.50 |
| Planning talents' career paths | 30.50 |
| Shaping the remuneration system for talents | 22.00 |
| Assessing talented employees | 26.50 |
| Employer branding | 12.50 |
| Creating project teams | 5.00 |

*Note*: Respondents could choose any applicable.

Reasons for taking action in the field of talent management originate both from the environment that an organisation operates within and from the inside, including those stemming from a specific mindset of managers. This is evidenced by the following quotes (Box 4.6).

---

**BOX 4.6 DRIVERS FOR INTRODUCING TALENT MANAGEMENT PRACTICES**

Activities related to talents arise from business necessity – you can't work without good people. With a small structure, it is still possible as the company is propelled by its owner, but then there is a critical moment in each company when responsibilities should be delegated. (Company Q)

We took action regarding talented employees primarily because we believe that everyone expects continuous development. Moreover, these people also want to be noticed and highlighted, and finally, they are human capital. We want to have them and retain them. They are our strong resources and it is what distinguishes us in the future. (Company J)

We took the first steps in this regard in 2015. Why? There are certainly several reasons. The two most important ones are competitiveness on the labour market in the IT industry in which we operate and the growing requirements of customers

*(Continued)*

---

which can be met if you have adequate staff. The idea of taking such actions came from the board. (Company P)

We want to keep talented employees as long as possible and appreciate them so as not to make the most important talents leave us. The market is changing; it is getting more and more difficult. We also have a young generation, which I think is aptly described as difficult. (Company M)

Our boss is a key person – he is interested in the issue of talents; he reads and thinks a lot about it. There were no external companies introducing talent-related activities. It's from inside the company. (Company R)

I was fished out as a talent by Microsoft, I was properly targeted and I started to do the same thing myself, namely I looked for talents, targeted them, developed them and then incorporated them into the company. This is how my company was created. I believe that the most important strengths of a company are people who know what they want to achieve in life. We achieve a lot on the basis of talented people, so we know that it is a very important part of our business. (Company G)

Actions directed at talented employees are initiated by various parties. Most often, people signal that there are interesting areas and training options. But we also see some areas worth improving where there are opportunities for us. So here, the department manager often indicates such things. (Company J)

An interesting research question was the issue of the relationship between the length of the talent management practice period and the tasks undertaken within the system. For this purpose, the surveyed SMEs were divided into three groups. The first group included companies that had used the talent management practice for one year, the second group were companies that had introduced such activities in the previous 2–5 years, and finally, the third group consisted of those companies where the system of talent management had been applied for at least six years. The results obtained in the research proved that with respect to the majority of the tasks listed in Table 4.7, this criterion was a differentiating factor. The largest percentage of companies performing the tasks was in the group of enterprises where the talent management practices had been implemented for the longest time. It amounted to: seeking talents outside an organisation (35.29%), identifying talents inside an organisation (58.82%), recruiting and selecting talents (38.24%), developing and training talents (41.18%), planning talents' career paths (32.35), shaping the remuneration system of talents (29.41%), assessing talented employees (41.18%), employer branding (26.47%) and creating project teams (11.76%). The aggregate percentage for all the implemented tasks in this group of enterprises amounted to 34.96%. By comparison, in the second group of companies (the implementation of the talent management system in the previous 2–5 years), it totalled 26.5% and finally, in the first group (the implementation of the system over the previous year), it totalled 23.39%.[1]

The above-mentioned results clearly indicate that a longer period of the implementation of talent management practices supports the development of specific practices in this area. This was particularly evident in the case of such tasks as seeking talents outside an organisation, identifying talents inside a company, shaping the remuneration system of talents, assessing talented employees, employer branding and creating project teams. Therefore, it can be assumed that companies need time to develop mature solutions in the area of talent management. Relatively small differences in the three groups occurred in relation to such tasks as recruiting and selecting talents, developing and training talents as well as planning talents' career paths. It can be postulated that this is mainly due to the situation on the labour market, which is characterised by an increasingly felt deficit with regard to labour supply and the characteristics of the Y generation, which attaches great importance to factors related to personal development, and which constitutes a key part of the supply on the labour market.

Another research issue was the question 'Do the roles and tasks presented in the previous section reflecting the nature of talented employees' work in the surveyed companies affect the talent management practices undertaken?' The main results of the analysis are presented below. Thus, with regard to seeking talents on the external labour market, no major differences were found as a result of the declared nature of talented employees' work. Exceptions are companies where talented employees do not have strictly assigned tasks and roles and they take on such tasks and roles that result from current conditions.

These companies, which constituted only 3.5% of the surveyed population, did not take any actions in terms of seeking talents from outside. In this group, however, the highest percentage of indications that talented employees were identified within an organisation was recorded at 85.71%. Other enterprises also indicated that this task was performed and the percentage of affirmative answers ranged from 33.33% to 50%. Their activity in terms of recruiting and selecting talents was at a similar level in particular groups of enterprises, which is expressed by the percentage of companies ranging from 31.58% to 50%. The exceptions here are the above-mentioned companies where talented employees do not have strictly assigned tasks and roles and which did not look for talented employees outside, which means that they did not carry out the task of recruitment and selection. In all the groups of the surveyed enterprises, tasks related to the development and training of employees were implemented. Companies that engaged in activities with regard to training and development ranged from 28.57% in the group of companies where tasks and roles were not strictly assigned to talented employees to 68.4% in those companies where they performed managerial tasks, thus their potential was widely exploited. The activity regarding planning career paths varied in particular groups of enterprises. The highest percentage (66.67%) of companies applying such solutions was recorded in the group of companies describing the nature of talented employees' work through the prism of tasks and the roles of mentors for other employees, as well as advisers of managers. It should be stressed, however, that such companies accounted only for 3% of the research sample. The second position was taken by companies that defined the character of talents' work as performing tasks consistent with their qualifications related to their job positions and occasionally also as undertaking other specialised tasks (e.g. coordination or control), for which the percentage was 37.84%. Finally, the third place was occupied by enterprises where the work of talents was referred to as performing usually specialised tasks in various areas, such as sales, logistics, finance and/or tasks related to the management of specialised processes (e.g. creating innovations, branding and promotion), which happened in 30.77% of the surveyed SMEs. It is worth emphasising here that these two groups had the largest share in the research group.

When it comes to shaping talents' remuneration systems, the number of companies undertaking such activities was relatively low, and large variations in particular groups could be observed. The largest percentage (42.11%) of enterprises performing this task occurred among those which defined the nature of talents' work as performing managerial functions that created wide opportunities to use their potential. In the subsequent places were companies where the character of talented employees' work was referred to as the implementation of specialised functions or the management of specialised processes (27.69%), followed by companies where their work was defined as mainly performing tasks corresponding to their qualifications and related to their position and sporadically undertaking other types of tasks (20.27%). Companies applying the practice of assessing talented employees in our survey constituted 50% and was usually undertaken in the group where the nature of talented employees' work was described as fulfilling the tasks and functions of mentors for other employees, as well as advisers of managers. As regards the group of companies defining the nature of talents' work through the prism of managing the implementation of specialised functions or managing specialised processes, it happened in 35.3% of the SMEs surveyed, while in the group of enterprises where the character of talented employees' work was referred to as performing tasks related to their qualifications/skills pertaining to their job positions, it happened in 44.3% of the SMEs.

Employer branding was found to be a less frequent activity than the other tasks in the surveyed SMEs (see Table 4.7). Companies that are active in this field were the ones in which talents' work was defined as performing managerial functions (21.05%) and in the group of enterprises where the nature of their work was defined as managing specialised functions or processes (20%). Finally, the task of creating teams carried out as part of the talent management system was undertaken most frequently by companies in which the character of talents' work was regarded as performing the function of mentors for employees and superiors. This happened in 16.67% of the SMEs surveyed. In the other groups of enterprises, this happened in no more than a few percent, and in the case of companies where there were no clearly assigned tasks for talents, this percentage was zero.

## Acquisition of Talents from Internal and External Sources

Acquiring talented employees is one of the basic talent management processes in an organisation. The following practices are used with respect to identifying talents within an organisation, attracting them from outside sources and choosing appropriate selection methods. Data contained in Table 4.7 indicates that the surveyed enterprises use both internal and external sources when they look

*Table 4.8* The ways of identifying talents inside an organisation

| | Share in % |
|---|---|
| The analysis of the level of achievement of goals in the previous year | 31.50 |
| The analysis of evaluation results from the previous year | 38.50 |
| The analysis of evaluation results from the last few years | 40.00 |
| Interviews with superiors about outstanding employees | 40.00 |
| Advertisements published on the intranet or other internal communication channels in a company | 25.50 |
| Organising development centre procedures | 19.50 |
| The evaluation of work results in project teams | 20.50 |
| The assessment of the competences of potential candidates with the use of the 360-degree feedback tool | 9.50 |
| Mentoring and coaching sessions | 5.50 |

*Note*: Respondents could choose any applicable.

for talented employees; however, the percentage of those indicating the use of internal sources was higher. Table 4.8 presents the results of research on activities undertaken to identify talents within an organisation. As can be seen from the cited data, the most commonly used methods of identifying talents within a company are the analyses of evaluation results from the last few years and information from superiors about outstanding employees. In both cases, such talent spotting happened 40% of the time. Almost as frequently used for the purpose of identifying talents is the analysis of evaluation results from the previous year (38.5%) as well as the level of achievement of goals in the previous year (31.5%).

The statements in Box 4.7 illustrate the approach to practices in the process of acquiring talented employees.

---

**BOX 4.7 PRACTICES IN TALENT ACQUISITION**

Activities aimed at acquiring talented employees are dictated by the market. We must acquire these people in various ways, through internal promotions or market activities. The current situation and the intensive development of the company means that we need new employees all the time. We have already used employees from other plants, from the outplacement programme, we place job advertisements and cooperate with the employment office. (Company H)

---

Recruitment is carried out in such a way that the people we hire are people with certain talents. At the recruitment stage, we ask about issues related to their approach to work. The job offer is formulated in such a way that a candidate knows what to expect. If such a person has the talent, then above all, this person is employed in a position consistent with his or her character, talents and personal predispositions. (Company K)

Acquiring talents from competitors is welcome. If a sales-person says that a department in another company is going to fall apart, we try to do something. It is a type of whispered recruitment. (Company M)

We mainly look for employees with experience when it comes to programmers, so I admit that we look for them in other companies. (Company F)

I graduated in 1992 and I started a company without any experience of working in other companies, but I had an idea of what I wanted it to be. All the people were hired by me, I wanted to talk to everyone. In this way, I wanted to match people to cultural features, I didn't just look at education. (Company Q)

The analysis of the methods used to identify talents within an organisation in accordance with the criterion of the period of the talent management system implementation showed that in the group of companies with the longest period of applying such practices (six or more years), it was observed that various ways of identifying talented employees were used. The aggregate percentage of all the methods of identifying talents amounted to 34.97%, while in the group of enterprises applying talent management practices for a period of from two to five years, it was applied in 24.97% instances. Finally, in companies that introduced the talent management system in the previous year, it happened 21.24% of the time.

The following methods of identifying talents were more frequently used in the group of companies that applied talent management system for the longest time, namely, the analysis of evaluation results from the previous year (50%), the analysis of evaluation results from the last few years (47.06%), the organisation of a development centre procedure (41.18%) and the evaluation of work in project teams (35.29%). The smallest differences in the three compared groups of enterprises occurred in relation to the use of interviews with superiors about outstanding employees as well as the intranet and other internal communication channels as methods of identifying talented employees.

Taking into consideration the nature of work entrusted to talented employees as a criterion for differentiating the use of specific ways of identifying talents, it turned out that the aggregate percentage for the application of all the methods was the highest in the group of companies defining the character of talents' work as performing managerial tasks (34.5%). By comparison, the above indicator in companies defining the nature of talents' work as the implementation of specialised tasks and/or the management of specific processes was 33.5%; in companies that described the nature of talents' work mainly through the prism of tasks regarding their qualifications related to their positions and also occasionally other specialised tasks related to coordination and control, this figure was 24.93%. In enterprises defining talents' tasks through the prism of merely performing tasks related to their qualifications/skills concerning their job positions, this indicator was at the level of 12.64%.

In the two groups of companies that achieved the highest total rate of the application of talent identification methods within an organisation, the following methods of acquiring talented employees were used more frequently than in the other groups: interviews with supervisors, the analyses of evaluation results from the last few years, advertisements on the intranet and other methods of internal communication, the assessment of teamwork performance as well as coaching and mentoring sessions. Above-average results were also obtained in the group of enterprises defining the nature of talented employees' work as the tasks and roles of mentors for other employees, as well as advisers of managers. However, one should bear in mind that the share of this group of companies in the research sample was small.

Table 4.9 contains data on activities undertaken in the surveyed enterprises that are focused on identifying talents on the external labour market. They show that the companies in question most often use various media, formulating high requirements for potential candidates in their search for talented individuals. Such activities were declared by 52.5% of the surveyed companies. Trade media or media related to a given area of activity is used by 37.5% of the companies. The use of employees' recommendations was at a similar level with the percentage of responses being 36.50%.

Analysing the above data following the criterion of the talent management implementation period, it turns out that the highest

*Table 4.9* The ways of identifying talents from outside an organisation

|  | Share in % |
|---|---|
| Posting standard job advertisements and selecting people who are regarded as potential talents from the pool of candidates | 32.50 |
| Posting job advertisements in various media, yet formulating very high requirements and expectations for candidates | 52.50 |
| Advertisements in the media related to particular sectors of industry or specific areas of activity | 37.50 |
| Using the recommendations of employees who are already employed in a company | 36.50 |
| Competitor analysis and the identification of people that a company would like to hire | 25.50 |
| Using the assistance of consulting companies that search for talented employees in other companies | 19.50 |
| Organising competitions and/or internship programmes for schools and university graduates | 11.00 |

*Note*: Respondents could choose any applicable.

aggregate percentage for activities used with regard to identifying talents from external sources was in the group of enterprises that had practiced talent management for the longest time (32.35%). In the other two groups, it was lower: 25.16% in the group of companies where the talent management system had been implemented from two to five years previously and 24.01% in the group applying talent management practices for one year.

With respect to the majority of methods used to seek talents outside an organisation, the largest share was taken by companies with the longest experience in the field of talent management, particularly for using employees' recommendations, identifying talents in rival companies and using consulting services.

Using the criterion of the nature of talented employees' work as the basis for analysing different ways of looking for and identifying talents outside an organisation, the following picture of the practices in the surveyed SMEs emerged.

The highest aggregate percentage of using all the identification methods was obtained in the group of enterprises defining the character of talents' work as managerial tasks and functions (36.84%). A similar level of this indicator was obtained in the group of companies defining the work of talented employees as the tasks and roles of mentors for other employees and advisers of people in managerial positions (33.33%), as well as in the group of companies defining it as performing mostly specialised tasks and functions and/or tasks concerning the management of specialised processes (33.19%). However, this indicator was clearly lower in the group of companies that defined the work of talented employees as only performing tasks that relate to their qualifications concerning their job positions (9.36%). The largest differences between the group of enterprises with the highest overall indicator of the use of talent identification methods applied outside of the company and the other groups occurred with respect to the following methods of identifying talents: placing standard job advertisements and selecting people recognised as talents (78.95%), using the services of consulting companies which search for talented employees in other enterprises (47.37%) and identifying talents in rival companies (42.11%).

Recruited candidates are assessed with the use of various selection techniques to determine whether they are suitable for particular job positions. The research indicates that the following selection tools are most commonly used: interviews (60.5%), practical exercises related to a position – such as role-playing and case studies (40.5%), practical exercises that are not related to the character of a position but developing general competences (37%), the initial analysis of applications (31.5%), knowledge tests (29%), the assessment centre method (22.4%), psychological tests (20.5%), analytical tests (19.5%) and language tests (7%). Based on the conducted research, the results of which are presented above, it can be stated that in the process of recruiting and then selecting talented employees, a fairly wide range of methods is used that are typical for human resource management.

Comparing the surveyed SMEs in terms of the period of applying talent management practices, it should be emphasised that the companies which had implemented such practices earlier had more frequently used various techniques for selecting talented employees.

The aggregate percentage for all selection techniques for this group was 35.26% compared to 25.79% in the group practising talent management for a period of 2–5 years and 21.83% for companies applying the talent management system for a year.

This is evidenced by the data below, which shows the percentage of companies using particular selection techniques in the group of enterprises implementing the talent management system for the period of six years or more: the initial analysis of applications (50%), interviews (73.53%), practical exercises related to a job position (41.18%), practical exercises that are not related to the character of a position (29.41%), the assessment centre method (38.24%), knowledge tests (35.29%), analytical tests (44.12%), psychological tests (41.18%) and language tests (14.71%). Only in the case of one technique, namely practical exercises not related to the character of a position, was the share of companies in this group lower than in the other two groups. The cited data shows that a longer period of applying talent management practices corresponds to the use of various selection techniques.

When we applied the criterion of the scope of tasks and functions performed by talents in the surveyed companies, the highest aggregate percentage of the use of various selection techniques was 34.5% and was recorded in the group of enterprises defining the nature of talented employees' work as performing managerial tasks. A slightly lower level of this indicator was obtained in the group of companies defining the work of specialised tasks and functions and/or tasks concerning the management of specialised processes (30.43%). By comparison, in those companies that referred to the character of their work as merely performing tasks consistent with the qualifications required for their job positions, the corresponding indicator was the lowest and amounted to 16.47%. In this last group, the most commonly used techniques were the initial analysis of applications (65.51%) and interviews (89.66%), while the remaining tools were used to a much lesser extent. The latter technique was also used most frequently in the group of companies defining talents' work as mainly performing tasks concerning their qualifications related to their positions but occasionally also other specialised tasks (71.62%). Practical exercises related to a job position as a selection technique were most often used in companies defining the nature of talents' work as usually performing specialised tasks and/or tasks related to the management of specialised processes (55.38%) and managerial tasks and functions (52.63%). In both groups of enterprises mentioned above, the assessment centre method was also most frequently used: 38.46% (specialised tasks) and 31.58% (managerial tasks) as well as knowledge tests at the levels of 38.46% (specialised tasks) and 36.84% (managerial tasks). The other selection techniques were used to the greatest extent by enterprises defining talents' work as managerial tasks and functions, and the breakup of tasks were as follows: practical exercises not related to the character of a job position (57.89%), competitions and internship programmes (31.58%), psychological tests (47.37%) and analytical tests (31.58%).

## Talent and Career Development

Talent development occupies a central place in human resource management, especially in relation to the group of employees recognised as talents in a given organisation, regardless of how the essence of talent is perceived. This is due to several reasons, first, due to their great importance for SMEs; second, because of increasing amounts of time and financial resources devoted to acquiring and retaining talents; finally, due to the significance that is attached to the development opportunities of employees from young generations who constitute an increasing share among professionally active people. In other words, development activities undertaken in enterprises are an important factor in enhancing talents' involvement and retention. The above issues were the subject of the authors' research, the results of which are presented below. It is worth recalling here that the share of companies declaring activities in the area of talent development was 41.5% (Table 4.7). Investing in the development of talented employees takes various forms, among which the most commonly used was training conducted by internal trainers and specialists (42%), closed training for employees (39%) and open training (35.5%). Based on the data contained in Table 4.10, it can be stated that in the surveyed enterprises, there are also other forms of training, such as workshops, coaching, case studies, project works and self-education; however, the scope of their application is rather limited.

*Table 4.10* Development activities targeted at talented employees

|  | *Share in %* |
| --- | --- |
| External, generally accessible training organised by external provider | 35.50 |
| Firm dedicated training organised by external provider | 39.00 |
| In-house training conducted by internal trainers or specialists | 42.00 |
| Workshops | 25.00 |
| Coaching programmes | 24.00 |
| Case studies | 23.50 |
| Project works | 20.50 |
| E-learning | 11.00 |
| Postgraduate studies | 13.00 |
| Courses with certificates | 27.50 |
| Self-study | 18.00 |

*Note*: Respondents could choose any applicable.

Comparing the surveyed SMEs in terms of the period of applying talent management, it should be emphasised that the companies which had implemented such practices earlier than others had more frequently adopted various forms of training. The aggregate percentage for all training forms for the group introducing talent management for six or more years was 43.33% compared to 19.42% in the group practising talent management for a period of 2–5 years and 18.5% for companies applying talent management for a year.

When we apply the criterion of the scope of tasks and functions performed by talents in the surveyed SMEs, the highest aggregate percentage of the use of various training forms was recorded in two groups of enterprises: those defining the nature of talented employees' work as specialised tasks and functions and/or tasks concerning the management of specialised processes (31.89%) and those defining the nature of talents' work as performing managerial functions (30.14%). By comparison, in those SMEs that referred to the character of talents' work as merely performing tasks consistent with the qualifications required for their job positions, the use of various forms of training was the lowest (17.55%).

Dedicated training programmes occupy a special place in the practice of developing talented employees. These types of solutions are used particularly in large companies. Therefore, the question arises of whether SMEs also use development training programmes. The results are presented in Table 4.11. They show that the vast majority of the surveyed enterprises use development programmes targeted at talented employees, as only 9% did not declare that such practices were applied. It is worth noting that half of the surveyed companies (50.5%) offer joint development programmes for the group of talented workers, individual development plans are offered by 11%, while 29.5% of companies implement development

*Table 4.11* Development programmes dedicated to talents

|  | Share in % |
| --- | --- |
| We offer standard development programmes for all employees | 29.50 |
| We offer special joint development plan for talents | 50.50 |
| We offer development plans created individually for each person | 11.00 |
| We do not offer development programmes for talents | 9.00 |

activities for talented employees as part of activities addressed to all of their employees.

The thematic scope of development programmes targeted at talented employees included the following issues:

- developing managerial competences in order to prepare for managerial roles – 55.5%;
- developing skills related to the character of a job position – 31.5%;
- deepening knowledge of the functioning of an organisation as a whole – 30.5%;
- expanding expert/specialist knowledge – 9.5%.

The statements in Box 4.8 illustrate additionally applied practices with regard to development activities.

---

**BOX 4.8  ADDITIONAL DEVELOPMENTAL ACTIVITIES FOR TALENTS**

We have two types of development projects. The first one is addressed to candidates who we recruit, and it is also used to find people with potential. The other one is for our employees and it covers two thematic areas to which employees can apply, namely a managerial programme for those who think about such a career and an expert programme for those who want to develop in this direction. Since the introduction of the talent management programme in 2015, it has been more individualised in terms of matching it to the potential of individual talents and the needs of the organisation. (Company P)

There is no development programme for talented employees, but they are sent for specialised training that can help in the development of such people. Other employees are not offered such training. The advantage for the company is that those trained talented employees transfer their knowledge to other employees. (Company R)

I really like the fact that if someone demonstrates his or her skills, then the boss does not stick rigidly to such standards as courses or education. Although, of course, we want our employees to be well-educated. And coming back to the career, it is possible to even go from rags to riches if someone really wants and tries hard. (Company I)

---

> Based on the observation of employees, their commitment, we try to develop them gradually. The problem is that companies train and then expect a return on their investment. And very often, young people learn quickly and then go higher, not necessarily in the same company. So, there is a fear that it will not be an investment, but a waste of money. (Company B)

From a cognitive point of view, it was interesting to examine possible differences in the approach to offering development programmes for talented employees depending on the talent management implementation period in the surveyed companies. Based on the research results, it was stated that joint development plans for talents were used to the greatest extent by enterprises that had implemented talent management practices during the previous year (54.39%). The joint development plans in the second group of companies applying talent management practices for 2–5 years were used to the extent of 53.21%, while in the third group of enterprises using talent management practices for six years and longer, it was lower (35.29%). In this last group of enterprises, individual development plans for talents were applied to a greater extent (23.53%). This was significantly higher than in the other groups, as it was 7.02% for the first group of companies and 9.17% for the second group. Moreover, research showed that in companies using talent management practices for the shortest time, the share of those that did not offer any development programmes for talented employees was the highest (15.79%).

Another research issue was to examine whether the way of assigning roles and tasks to talented employees diversified the approach to development programmes. The most important conclusions in this regard are presented below. First of all, it is noteworthy that in the group of enterprises that defined the character of talents' work as performing merely tasks related to their qualifications/skills concerning their job positions, the share of companies where development programmes were addressed to all employees was the highest (55.17% of indications). Also in this group, the percentage of companies that did not offer development programmes for talents was the highest (24.14%). Second, in the most represented group of SMEs, where the nature of talented employees' work was described as performing specialised tasks/functions and/or tasks related to the management of specialised processes, the percentage of companies offering joint development plans for talents was high (67.69%). In the group of enterprises where the nature of talents' work was defined as performing managerial functions, joint development plans for talents were offered at a similar level (63.16%). Individual development plans were also offered in both groups; however, the latter group offered them more (21.05%) compared to the former group (16.92%). The quoted data proves that the character of work entrusted to talented employees in an organisation affects the approach to development programmes. In companies where the nature of talents' work was described as specialised and managerial tasks, talented development programmes – both joint and individual – were more often implemented.

Career management is a significant element of activity undertaken in the area of talent development. As a preliminary remark, it is worth referring to the data contained in Table 4.7 that show that among the tasks performed as part of talent management, career planning was declared by 30.5% of the surveyed companies. However, when asked whether the talented employees were specifically considered in the career management/development processes, 57.5% of the surveyed companies answered 'yes' and 42.5% 'no'. This specificity is expressed in building individual career paths (27%), developing their passions and interests (25.5%) and individualising the pace and specific development techniques (5%).

Taking into account the period of talent management practice as a criterion for differentiating the approach to the above issues, it should be stated that among the companies that took into account the specificity of talents in career management, the group of enterprises which had practiced talent management for 2–5 years did it to a higher extent than others (65.14%). For comparison, it is worth adding that in the group of enterprises applying the talent management system for six or more years, 58.82% of SMEs added talent specificity to career management, while among companies that implemented talent management during the previous year, it was the lowest (42.11%).

Taking into consideration the character of work assigned to talents as a criterion for differentiating the approach to career management, it was established that the largest percentage of companies taking into account the specific nature of talents in career management was in the group of enterprises that defined the nature of talents' work as performing managerial tasks. In this group, 89.47% of companies declared the above fact, followed by companies defining the character of talented employees' work as the implementation of specialised tasks and/or the management of specific processes (66.15%). The third position was taken by companies defining talents' work mainly through the prism of tasks related to their qualifications and job positions but sporadically also other specialised tasks related to coordinating and controlling (63.51%). The obtained results confirm a conclusion arrived at earlier regarding the dedicated development programmes. In this case, it means that the nature of work entrusted to talents affects the approach to career management. In SMEs in which the character of work assigned to talented employees is associated with specialised and managerial tasks, the share of companies that take into account the specificity of talents in the practice of career management is greater.

## Assessing and Rewarding Talents

Among tasks performed within the scope of managing talented employees, the tasks of assessing and shaping remuneration systems for this group of employees were undertaken relatively less frequently, as evidenced by a rather small percentage of companies declaring such practices, which was at the level of 26.5% for assessment and 22% for remuneration (see Table 4.7). However, when respondents were asked whether the specificity of talented employees was included in the assessment system, 59.5% of them answered in the affirmative. There is a certain discrepancy here between the percentage of companies identifying talent assessment as a separate task in the talent management system (26.5%) and the percentage of indicators that the specificity of talents is included in the assessment system (59.5%). This may be due to the fact that in many SMEs, there are no dedicated talent assessment systems. The assessment of talented employees is made within the framework of a common evaluation system for all employees. Addressing the specificity of talents in assessment systems concerned performance evaluation criteria (32% of responses), competence evaluation criteria (20% of responses), assessment techniques (20% of responses), evaluators (10.5% of responses) and assessment frequency (3.5% of responses). To the largest extent, it occurred in the group of enterprises using talent management practices over the period of 2 to 5 years, which reflects the percentage of companies including the specificity of talents in assessment systems (69.72%). The percentage was only slightly lower in companies applying talent management practices for six or more years (61.76%), while it was the lowest in the group of enterprises applying the talent management system for one year (38.6%).

Considering the nature of talented employees' work as a criterion differentiating the approach discussed here for including the specificity of talents in evaluation systems, it should be noted that the majority of companies confirming such practices were recorded in the group of enterprises that defined talents' work as performing managerial functions (78.95%). The second position was taken by the group in which the character of talented people's work was referred to as mainly performing tasks related to their qualifications concerning given job positions, although occasionally also undertaking other specialised tasks (71.2%). Finally, in the third group, where talents' work was described as usually performing specialised tasks and/or tasks related to the management of specialised processes, such evaluation was done to the extent of 66.15%. For the sake of comparison, for companies that include the specificity of talents in their evaluation systems, in the group of enterprises defining the nature of talents' work as only performing tasks consistent with their qualifications required for their job position, the percentage was low (13.79%).

As in the case of assessing talented employees, the percentage of companies declaring the incorporation of specificity of talents into their remuneration systems (61.5%) was higher than the percentage of companies (presented in Table 4.7) declaring performing the task of shaping talent remuneration systems as part of talent management (22%). This discrepancy can be explained in a similar way as in the case of assessment, specifically by the fact that SMEs do not create dedicated talent remuneration systems; they try to introduce certain differentiating elements to remuneration systems common for all employees. Including the specificity of talents in shaping the system of remuneration concerned such elements as awards and bonuses (29%), the forms of remuneration (26.5%), rates of pay (22.5%) and benefits and allowances (8%). Including specificity of talents in rewarding practices occurred to the greatest extent among enterprises applying talent management practices for the longest time (70.59%). This practice occurred to the extent of 68.81% in companies that had introduced talent management in the period of from two to five years previously and finally in 42.11% in companies implementing talent management for one year.

Using the nature of talents' work as a criterion for differentiating the approach to the inclusion of specific nature of talents in remuneration systems, it turned out that the majority of companies confirming use of such a practice were those defining the nature of talented employees' work as performing managerial functions

(84.21%). The second place was taken by companies where the nature of talents' work was primarily regarded as the performance of tasks related to the qualifications required for a given job position, but sporadically also undertaking other specialised tasks (74.32%). Among enterprises defining the nature of talented people's work as typically performing specialised tasks and/or tasks related to managing specialised processes, the corresponding percentage was 63.08%. By comparison, for companies that take into consideration the specific nature of talented employees in remuneration systems, in the group of companies defining talents' work as only performing tasks consistent with their qualifications required for particular job positions, the percentage was low (17.24%).

The quotes in Box 4.9 additionally illustrate different approaches to the issue of talents remuneration.

---

**BOX 4.9  REMUNERATION FOR TALENTS**

For sure, the salaries of talented employees are higher. They are more committed people whose results show greater value. These people often receive some extra bonuses in the form of cash prizes or non-wage benefits. We are also working on some new ideas for benefits. We have a lot of young people, so we are looking for such paths that would suit them best. (Company E)

This is a company that is supposed to make money. We look at bonuses through the prism of performing tasks. If they are performed well and the goals are achieved then there is a bonus system. (Company K)

The modifications mainly concerned the motivation system so that it would effectively influence talent retention. Employees perform various tasks and they do what they like. They receive a part of their income from their own project, or they receive an additional prize or a block of shares. There is also praise and some privileges (training, trips). In general, it can be said that the atmosphere is humane, homely, friendly and family like. (Company G)

When it comes to remuneration, it is one of the best systems compared to other language schools, because there are high rates for lessons, bonuses for exceptional achievements and for parents' satisfaction. We have a diverse work assessment system. It is known that you use praise and money. There is nothing else you can think of here. (Company N)

---

On the basis of the above considerations, one may be tempted to draw the conclusion that in both areas discussed here (the assessment and remuneration of talented employees) similar trends occurred. Even though the percentage of SMEs with dedicated assessment and remuneration systems for talented employees is relatively low, most of them take into account the specificity of talents in their systems. Moreover, the percentage of companies applying this practice is higher among those that had implemented the talent management system earlier than among those that did so in the previous year. Similarly, the manner of determining the tasks and roles performed by talented employees which characterise the nature of their work is a factor differentiating the approach to the systems of assessment and remuneration. Among enterprises where the work of talented employees involves performing the tasks and roles of managers and specialists, the share of those taking into account the specific nature of talents is definitely higher than among enterprises where the work of talented people involves performing only tasks corresponding to their qualifications relating to their job positions.

## Addressing Talents' Expectations

One of the conditions for the effectiveness of activities taken within the framework of talent management aiming at building commitment among talented employees and retaining them in an organisation is the proper recognition of their expectations, the consideration of these expectations in the implementation of particular tasks and preparing an attractive offer of benefits for this group of employees (talent value proposition). Table 4.12 contains answers to the question: Does the company identify and take into account the expectations of talented employees?

*Table 4.12* Addressing talents' expectations

|  | *Share in %* |
| --- | --- |
| Internal transfers and promotions | 82.50 |
| Motivating factors | 79.50 |
| Remuneration | 73.50 |
| Development needs | 71.50 |
| Career pace and direction | 61.00 |
| The methods and organisation of work | 77.00 |
| Challenges | 63.50 |
| Work autonomy | 53.50 |

*Note*: Respondents could choose any applicable.

As can be seen from the data cited in the above table, the surveyed SMEs declare that they examine and consider talented employees' expectations. With respect to all types of expectations listed in Table 4.12, the number of companies that indicated such practices exceeded half of the sample. This turned out to be the highest in relation to internal transfers and promotions (82.5%) and motivating factors (79.5%), while the lowest related to work autonomy (53.5%).

It is worth noting that the practice of taking into consideration the expectations of talented employees was the most common in the group of enterprises implementing a talent management system for the longest time, that is, at least six years. This is confirmed by the high percentage of companies following this practice:

- internal transfers and promotions – 91.18%;
- motivating factors – 97.06%;
- remuneration – 97.06%;
- development needs – 97.06%;
- career pace and direction – 73.53%;
- the ways and the organisation of work – 91.18%;
- challenges – 73.53;
- work autonomy – 70.59%.

The aggregate percentage for all the above-mentioned practices was high (86.39%). In the other two groups of SMEs, the above indicators were at lower levels. With regard to companies applying a talent management system over a period of 2–5 years, the percentage of SMEs in the survey that took into account talent's expectations ranged from 87.16% (internal transfers and promotions) to 55.96% (work autonomy). The aggregate percentage for all practices with regard to addressing talents' expectations was 73.28%. For companies that had introduced talent management practices in the previous year, the corresponding percentage ranged from 68.42% (internal transfers and promotions) to 38.60% (working autonomy). The aggregate percentage for all practices with regard to addressing talent' expectations was 55.92%.

Using the nature of talented employees' work as a criterion for differentiating the approach to identifying and including talents' expectations in shaping the nature of particular tasks within the talent management system, the obtained data confirms that the largest percentage of companies using this practice occurred in three groups, which defined the nature of talents' work as follows:

- primarily performing tasks related to qualifications required for given job positions but also occasionally undertaking other specialised tasks (the aggregate percentage for all responses was 76.86%);
- performing managerial tasks and functions (the aggregate percentage for all responses was 76.32%);
- performing typically specialised tasks and/or tasks related to the management of specialised processes (the aggregate percentage for all responses was 73.85%).

As shown, the differences between the above three groups of enterprises were small. However, the sum of all indications in the group of enterprises referring to the nature of talented employees' work only on tasks consistent with their qualifications required for their job positions was clearly lower – 53.02% (the aggregate percentage for all responses).

A detailed analysis of data concerning addressing talents' expectations in particular groups of enterprises reveals a diverse picture of the practices used. Below is some data illustrating the observed trends. With regards to the area of internal transfers and promotions, the highest percentage of companies taking into account talents' expectations occurred in the group of enterprises defining their work through the prism of tasks and managerial functions (94.74%). In the area of motivating factors, talented workers' expectations were taken into consideration by the largest number of companies in the group defining the nature of their work as performing primarily tasks related to their qualifications required for given job positions but also sporadically undertaking other specialised tasks (86.49%). Similar percentages were recorded in the group of companies defining talents' work as managerial tasks and functions (84.21%) and in the group of companies that described the talents as performing mostly specialised tasks and/or tasks related to managing specialised processes (83.08%). Regarding the issue of remuneration, the highest share of companies considering talents' expectations was recorded in the group of companies describing talented employees' work as managerial tasks and functions (78.95%) and in the group of companies defining it as usually performing specialised tasks and/or tasks related to the management of specialised processes (78.46%). In the area of development needs, talents' expectations were taken into account to the greatest extent in the group of enterprises specifying the nature of talented employees' work as performing managerial tasks and functions (84.21%). It should be noted here that a 100% result occurred in the group of companies defining the nature of talents' work as the tasks and roles of mentors for other employees and advisers of people in managerial positions. However, due to its limited size (3%), any conclusions should be drawn with caution. In the area of career pace and direction, the largest percentage of enterprises considering talents' expectations occurred in the group of companies defining talented employees' work as executing managerial tasks and functions (78.95%). Regarding the methods and the organisation of work, talented workers' expectations were most often taken into consideration among companies specifying the character of their work as mainly performing tasks related to the qualifications required for given job positions but occasionally also as undertaking other specialised tasks (87.84%). In this group of enterprises, the percentage of companies including talents' expectations in the area of challenges (77.03%) and work autonomy (63.51%) was also the highest.

The quotes in Box 4.10 illustrate the practices applied with reference to employees' expectations.

---

**BOX 4.10 ADDRESSING TALENTS' EXPECTATIONS**

The management model is constantly changing and evolving towards greater decision making for employees and creating more space for them to act. This is something that motivates them because they see their influence. However, not everyone expects more decision making – some of them want to be experts while some want to be able to influence something bigger. The model went in the direction of cooperation, a model of partnership cooperation. (Company J)

We do not examine the level of satisfaction. Every week or twice a week we have meetings where all members sit and talk, what is cool and what is not, what they would like to change. They have courage and a chance to say it. (Company A)

We do not examine satisfaction. I used to care more about such things. On my part, I try to ensure a good salary, a good atmosphere at work and good working conditions. They

*(Continued)*

---

affect satisfaction, especially the atmosphere. In the area of workplace organisation, we implement a work–life balance policy, i.e. flexible forms of employment and flexible working hours, and employees are satisfied with that. (Company K)

To sum up the considerations presented above, the following can be noted:

- First, the process of identifying and taking into consideration the expectations of talented employees occurs in the group of surveyed SMEs.
- Second, the scope of identifying and taking into account expectations of talents varies in particular task areas where talented employees' expectations can be expressed.
- Third, an impact of the time factor on the practice of identifying and taking into consideration talents' expectations was noted – companies applying the talent management system for a longer time implemented such practices more often.
- Fourth, the nature of work performed by talented employees was a determining factor in identifying and considering the expectations of talents; companies determining the character of their work through the prism of specialised and managerial tasks and functions were more frequently active in this regard.

## Note

1 The aggregate percentage was applied to show to what extent particular talent management practices are used in different groups of examined companies.

# 5 Outcomes Reported by Small and Medium Enterprises That Introduced Talent Management Practices

The issues discussed in Chapter 1 prove that talented employees play a crucial role in ensuring the achievement of firms' goals. The importance of talents stems from both their unique abilities, skills and knowledge and from their potential to introduce innovative, non-standard actions in diverse job-related situations. Thus, it can be assumed that the application of particular talent-orientated activities should result in providing organisations with an opportunity to achieve the expected level of effectiveness. Despite the fact that talent-related issues have been investigated for three decades, research on the relationship between talent management practices and firms' performance is scarce. There are publications confirming the interdependence between talent management in general and performance, and between talent management and particular performance indicators (e.g. psychological contract and turnover intention). The lack of complex research is due to limitations stemming from the characteristics of the samples. Most of the research is conducted in large multinational organisations; this makes it very difficult to isolate the impact of talent management on overall performance. However, there are many papers and publications confirming that implementing specific, adjusted to best practices and standardised human resource activities enhance firms' effectiveness and competitive advantage. An example of such research was conducted by Sheehan (2014), according to which specific HRM interventions have an impact upon SMEs' performance. The interdependence between HRM practices and the effectiveness of organisations was proven by Jiang et al. (2012) who confirmed that HRM practices have a positive impact on financial performance by both increasing the value of human capital and supporting desired employee behaviours. In particular, they concluded that the skill-enhancing and motivation-enhancing practices are of the highest importance in this case. Thus, it can be claimed that talent management, which encompasses practices targeting key employees has a positive impact upon not only knowledge and skills development but also on motivation, organisational commitment and extra-role behaviours. Such attitudes imply an increase in individual performance, which, in turn, enables organisations to meet or even exceed their goals (Collings & Mellahi, 2009).

The effects of HRM practices can be assessed with the use of three perspectives: financial, organisational and HR-related (Dyer & Reeves, 1995). When taking into account the financial perspective, it is assumed that by applying HRM practices, organisations are able to realise their expected goals and reduce operational costs at the same time, which in turn increases the organisation's profit level. This is achieved by, for example, hiring well-qualified employees who are strongly dedicated to task fulfilment. Additionally, providing employees with developmental opportunities, allowing them to make job-related decisions and promoting innovativeness support the improvement of task-performing schemes and methods. This can lead to modifications in internal processes that are related to the organisational effectiveness perspective. The last perspective concerning HR-related outcomes is related to their effects on both the internal and external labour markets. When evaluating the effectiveness of HRM practices, the employer brand, retention level, turnover intentions, motivation and organisational commitment can be evaluated.

The research conducted by Sheehan (2014) confirmed that some of the HRM activities have a direct but unequal impact upon SMEs' performance and differ with regard to the three above-mentioned perspectives. For example, *strategic people management, recruitment and selection, training and development* and *compensation* were the most important HRM practices for financial performance. *Strategic people management, recruitment and selection, training and development* and *employee voice or consultation and information sharing* were most the impactful practices with regard to innovation, which refers to the organisational perspective. In the third perspective, HR-related outcomes, the labour turnover was investigated in Sheehan's research. *Strategic people management, recruitment and selection, performance appraisal* and *training and development* were HRM practices which positively impact the outcomes in this perspective.

In Bethke-Langenegger et al.'s (2011) research, an association between HRM practices and organisational performance was also confirmed when taking into account talent management practices only. On the basis of activities undertaken by the investigated companies, the authors grouped them into four categories of firms including those which focus on *corporate strategy, succession planning, attracting and retaining talents* and *developing talents*. According to their findings, it can be stated that talent management practices with a strong *focus on corporate strategy* have a statistically significant, positive impact on corporate profit. The approach which aims at supporting *succession planning* has the weakest impact on organisational performance, particularly on non-financial outcomes at both the organisational and the human resource level. The strategy focusing on *attracting and retaining talents* has the greatest effect on HR outcomes. The focus on *developing talents* has a statistically significant, positive effect on almost all of the performance indicators reviewed. However, it should be added that in this research the sample comprised only 17% SMEs.

Similar conclusions to those above, although only with regard to the financial perspective, were drawn by Glaister, Karacay, Demirbag and Tatoglu (2018). They found that talent management practices were associated with firm performance and *defining special tasks to stimulate learning, organising work in project teams, networking, in-house development programmes, coaching and mentoring, cross-disciplinary working* and *formal career plans* had the strongest relationship with performance.

Applying the conclusions of Khoreva et al. (2017), it can be stated that talent management practices should expand the capacity of high-potential employees; support favourable attitudes and behaviours that can result in superior performance; facilitate greater commitment; increase motivation to work; support organisational effectiveness and create conditions for enhancing employees' agility in responding to the challenges of modern business.

In the theoretical model (see Chapter 2), it is assumed that talent management practices have a positive impact upon firm's financial, organisational and HR-related outcomes. On the basis of the research referring to the interdependence between HRM and talent management practices and performance, it can be acknowledged that acquiring highly skilled candidates, developing employees' competences and creating motivational systems enhance employee commitment and raises profits and sales level. Moreover, because talent management practices increase the value of human capital, they may also result in higher innovativeness of a particular SME. These practices enable the introduction of new products and services and the improvement of those already existing in accordance with customer expectations. The possible effects of talent management programmes may also concern SMEs' internal systems. Such organisations change or widen their internal systems as a result of new knowledge acquisition. The last category of outcomes corresponds to the image of SMEs on the internal as well as the external labour market. Organisations that value talents and introduce appropriate talent management practices are perceived as those creating a better and more customised work environment. Thus, they more often become employers of choice. Moreover, having the possibility to participate in talent management programmes increases employee satisfaction, which helps to retain talents, strengthens their organisational commitment and leads to higher performance.

## Overview of the Outcomes Reported by the Investigated Enterprises

### *Business Outcomes*

The gathered data confirms that, in general, the investigated companies report business outcomes to be at a more than satisfactory level. There are only a few companies in the sample that claim to suffer from negative trends with regard to the analysed business performance indicators.

Of all the indicators, the *number of customers* is most frequently highlighted as the outcome with the most positive trends. As many as 42.5% of respondents claim that they have noticed an increase in the *number of customers* within the last five years and 38% claim that it has remained stable. *Brand recognition* is observed at similar levels: 42% declare an increase while 41.5% claim that it has remained stable. The third positively evaluated indicator is *products and services sales value*, which has increased in 41.5% of companies and remained stable in 33%. However, it should be stated that barely one out of every five companies (18%) has noticed a decrease in the *value of products and services sales* level (see Table 5.1).

Less positive trends can be ascribed to *products and services sales volume*. As many as 14% of the investigated companies claim that the number of products and services sold has decreased within the last five years and in 42.5% of cases, it has remained stable. A similar situation refers to the *overall financial condition*. Of the investigated companies, 14% claim they have noticed a decrease and in 40%, it has remained stable.

*Table 5.1* Changes appearing in business outcome indicators over the previous five years

| | Share in % | | | | | |
|---|---|---|---|---|---|---|
| | *Definitely decreased* | *Rather decreased* | *Remained stable* | *Rather increased* | *Definitely increased* | *Do not know* |
| Product/services sales volume | 5.50 | 9.50 | 42.50 | 24.50 | 11.50 | 6.50 |
| Product/services sales value | 2.50 | 15.50 | 33.50 | 29.50 | 12.00 | 7.00 |
| Profit level | 4.00 | 6.50 | 40.50 | 31.00 | 8.50 | 9.50 |
| Number of customers | 3.50 | 8.50 | 38.00 | 31.00 | 11.50 | 7.50 |
| Overall financial condition | 2.50 | 11.50 | 40.00 | 27.00 | 11.50 | 7.50 |
| Brand recognition | 2.50 | 7.50 | 41.50 | 28.50 | 13.50 | 6.50 |

On the basis of this data, it can be concluded that the product/service per customer ratio is decreasing in the investigated companies. These companies claim to have more customers but sell them fewer products. However, the analysis of aggregated data confirms that these companies are doing well in general, as only 5% confirm a decrease and 11% confirm an increase in all the investigated indicators.

The quotes in Box 5.1 confirm the positive business outcomes in SMEs that have implemented talent management.

---

**BOX 5.1  BUSINESS OUTCOMES IN SMES THAT HAVE IMPLEMENTED TALENT MANAGEMENT PRACTICES**

Yes, we have introduced new services recently. The costs level remains stable but incomes have doubled within the last year. (Company A)

Definitely yes, we are better recognised on the international market, the number of customers has increased, and we have entered the stock exchange, which allowed us to get additional funds for company development. (Company G)

*(Continued)*

---

Definitely yes, next year we are planning to increase production by 50%. Every year we set higher goals, we enter new markets, and we set business relationships with new customers. (Company H)

Yes, the sales level has increased, we have introduced new services and we get engaged more frequently in international cooperation. The number of customers has not increased, but we do not want it to rise. We select our customers because we continuously receive some business proposals and there are many opportunities. (Company E)

Yes, the firm's overall condition is very good. There are positive changes in the market range, the number of services we offer and the number of customers. Additionally, we have lowered the costs of running a business, we have introduced some new processes and negotiated better terms of cooperation with suppliers. (Company I)

### Organisational Outcomes

The analysis of organisational outcomes was conducted with the use of indicators referring to changes in products and services provided by the organisations, changes in technology used, changes in internal processes and market image.

Modifications or improvements in products and services have been introduced in two out of every three companies (66.5%) within the last five years (see Table 5.2). However, only 10% of the

*Table 5.2* Changes in products/services and in technology

|  | *Share in %* |
|---|---|
| Our products/services have not been submitted to any changes since they were launched. | 33.50 |
| We have introduced minor changes and modifications to the initial versions of our products/ services. | 56.50 |
| We have introduced significant changes in our products/ services; they significantly vary from their initial versions. | 10.00 |
| We have not implemented any changes in our technology since it was introduced. | 33.50 |
| We have introduced new solutions and applied changes in technology used. | 56.00 |
| We have significantly changed technology; it differs from the initial version. | 10.50 |

*Note*: Respondents could choose any applicable.

companies claim that they have introduced significant changes and 56.5% report minor modifications or improvements. Almost the same share of companies have introduced either significant or minor changes in the technology they use to produce goods or provide services.

As stated in Table 5.2, one out of every three companies states it has not introduced any changes in the technology or in the products or services they offer.

A higher level of organisational outcomes can be identified when taking into account internal processes (see Table 5.3); nearly one out of every four SMEs (26.5%) claim they do not modify their internal processes. Most frequently, the investigated companies introduced changes to some extent (48%), and in 23% of cases, the companies have modified their internal systems significantly in order to adapt to current business needs. Additionally, within the last five years, 2.5% of SMEs have changed their internal processes, introduced new processes and created a complex system that supports running a business.

Analysis of the gathered data made it possible to conclude that the image of investigated companies is based on factors that are crucial for building a sustainable competitive advantage. The factors most frequently indicated are as follows: *industry-specific experience* (47.5%), *high quality of products/services* (36%) and *social responsibility of a company* (36%). Moreover, 30.5% of SMEs claimed they are perceived as a *trustworthy company*. Such factors mostly refer to relational (customer) capital, which cannot be created on the basis of short-term activities. Thus, it can be concluded that the role of intangible resources is important in building an SME's competitive position. Additionally, only 13% of the investigated companies declare that they are identified as a company offering the cheapest products and services. Thus, it is the minority of companies which apply low-price strategies to increase their market share (see Table 5.4).

*Table 5.3* Changes in internal processes

|  | Share in % |
|---|---|
| No, we use the same process as we introduced initially. | 26.50 |
| We have changed them to some extent. | 48.00 |
| We have introduced significant changes to adapt internal systems to our current needs. | 23.00 |
| We have changed them and we have introduced some new processes to create a complex system that supports running a business. | 2.50 |

*Table 5.4* Perceived market image

|  | Share in % |
|---|---|
| As a company with experience in the industry/on the market | 47.50 |
| As a provider of high-quality products/services | 36.00 |
| As a socially responsible company | 36.00 |
| As a trustworthy company | 30.50 |
| As a technology leader in the industry | 26.00 |
| As a stable company, well-grounded on the market | 25.50 |
| As an employer of choice | 22.50 |
| As an innovative company | 20.00 |
| As a flexible company, adjusting to customers' needs | 15.50 |
| As a company offering the cheapest products and services | 13.00 |
| It is hard to say how we are perceived on the market | 7.00 |

*Note*: Respondents could choose any applicable.

On the basis of the conducted analysis, it can be concluded that the vast majority of investigated companies confirmed the existence of positive trends in indicators referring to organisational outcomes. Two out of every three companies have introduced modifications in the products/services they offer and in the technology they use. Nearly three out of every four companies have improved, either slightly or significantly, their internal processes. They are also focused on building their competitive position on the basis of intangible resources, which is proven by the significance of industry-specific experience (referring to know-how), high quality of products and services (referring to organisational capital) and trust as well as social responsibility (which refers to relational capital).

Qualitative research confirmed that investigated SMEs have implemented many changes in the way they operate. In general, they perceive themselves as being very innovative (see Box 5.2).

---

**BOX 5.2  CHANGES IN THE WAY SMES OPERATE**

Our firm is highly innovative. We are continuously developing with regard to sales quantity, geographical coverage and the technology we use. Innovations relate to enhancing products/ services and to the technology we use to provide services to customers. (Company R)

Innovativeness in our firm is on a very high level. We have been praised several times within projects co-financed by EU funds. (Company G)

We are innovative, we have completed a complex investment in a new production system – it was aimed at widening our offer. Now we are launching a new product on the market. (Company O)

We are very innovative. In 2018, we were honoured by the London Stock Exchange as a one of 1,000 companies that inspire Europe. There were only 30 companies from Poland. (Company H)

The innovations introduced enhance not only technology but also other internal processes. This is proven by the quotes in Box 5.3.

## BOX 5.3 TYPES OF INTRODUCED INNOVATIONS

Innovations refer to our managing system – well, I would not even call it managing, it is self-navigating, and self-organising. Our employees work when there is something to do, if there are only a few tasks to fulfil they may even not show up in the office. Additionally, I do not control them, they know what to do and when to do it. (Company A)

Our innovations mostly refer to production and the technology used, but they also apply to internal processes. We have introduced Lean principles, which definitely helped us to increase efficiency. (Company H)

We may talk about innovations in the services we offer – they were the foundation of strategic renewal after the collapse in 2016. In creating these services, talents were fully engaged. We have also introduced some innovations in research methodology, in the selling process and in managing the sales team. (Company P)

We introduce innovations mainly in technology relating to providing services and creating products. Behind every innovation, there is a certain amount of money that needs to be

*(Continued)*

spent. Thus, we focus only on activities that can bring the expected return on investment. We do not develop supportive departments and processes, I believe we could, but this is not our core business. We need to be one step ahead of our competitors in IT. (Company M)

Innovations refer to all our activities. There is a huge number of modifications in internal processes. We constantly try to enhance cooperation, rewarding systems or the way we manage our employees. Innovations are also aimed at our relationships with our customers and the services we provide. (Company J)

### HR-Related Outcomes

To evaluate how talent management practices may impact upon HR-related outcomes, the investigated companies were asked to evaluate changes in employment, employee engagement, employer brand (perception of employees and candidates for employment) and potential difficulties in staffing.

The highest share of companies claim there have not been any changes in the employment level within the last five years. However, one out of every three companies (34%) declares an increase in the number of employees, while 13.5% had to make some workers redundant. On the basis of this information, it can be concluded that the investigated companies have the potential to grow.

The majority of respondents (59%) evaluate their employee engagement in fulfilling tasks as high – 11% claim it is very high and all employees are dedicated to work; 48% claim that most employees are highly dedicated to task fulfilment (see Table 5.5). Additionally, only 9.5% evaluate the level of engagement as low or very low. Thus, it can be stated that the introduced HR practices in these companies support the desired behaviours and attitudes of employees.

On the basis of the gathered data, it is impossible to develop a coherent image of the investigated companies based on the employees' perspective (see Table 5.6). The most frequently mentioned features of SMEs are *friendly climate* (37.5%), the *possibility to fulfil interesting tasks* (37.5%), *developmental opportunities* (31%) and the *possibility to be involved in the execution of diverse projects* (29%). Interestingly, as many as 17.5% of respondents claim they are perceived as an organisation which is *flexible and can adjust*

*Table 5.5* Assessment of employee engagement

|  | Share in % |
|---|---|
| Very high, all employees are highly engaged in their task fulfilment | 11.00 |
| Rather high, most employees are highly engaged in fulfilling their tasks | 48.00 |
| Moderate, some employees are highly engaged but others perform their tasks at the minimum level | 31.50 |
| Rather low, most employees are not engaged in task fulfilment | 9.00 |
| Very low, there are only a few employees who are engaged in task fulfilment | 0.50 |

*Table 5.6* Perceived employer brand: employees' perspective

|  | Share in % |
|---|---|
| As a company with a friendly organisational climate | 37.50 |
| As a company in which interesting tasks can be fulfilled | 37.50 |
| As a company providing developmental opportunities | 31.00 |
| As a firm in which one can be involved in the execution of diverse projects | 29.00 |
| As a firm offering attractive working conditions | 24.50 |
| As a company offering jobs that are adjusted to employees' competences | 23.00 |
| As a company offering competitive salaries | 23.00 |
| As a flexible organisation, adjusting to employees' expectations and needs | 17.50 |
| Our employees do not perceive us in any unique way and do not attribute any specific features to us | 16.00 |

*Note*: Respondents could choose any applicable.

*to employees' expectations and needs.* – the share seems quite high as SMEs tend to be perceived as those offering a high level of employee orientation.

The data presented in Table 5.6 implies that the employer brand of the investigated SMEs is built mainly on the basis of the diverse and wide range of tasks offered to employees, the developmental opportunities and the informal, friendly working conditions. Such characteristics are in line with the general image of SMEs. They are perceived as companies in which there is a low level of job formalisation and structuration, and in which many activities result from emerging needs. However, the above features of the investigated companies' employer brand are contrary to the image of SMEs, which was developed on the basis of respondents' answers referring to the context of talent management (see Chapter 3). When answering the questions concerning the general image of SMEs as employers, respondents claimed that these companies are perceived as companies in which there is a friendly climate, which are flexible and can adjust to employees' needs and expectations and which provide employees with an opportunity to fulfil a diverse scope of tasks and involvement in diverse projects. The first feature (friendly climate) was highlighted as the feature defining employer brand by 37.5% of investigated companies. The second (flexibility) was selected by only 17.5% and the third (a variety of tasks and projects) is available in only 29% of the investigated companies. Thus, it can be concluded that the investigated companies do not act proactively in building employer brand within their organisations. This may result in lowering the effectiveness of the undertaken HRM initiatives.

On the basis of the gathered data, it can also be concluded that the investigated companies do not have a strong brand on the labour market (see Table 5.7). Only 17.5% of the companies claim they are perceived as an employer of choice and candidates apply for jobs without vacancies being advertised. In merely half of the cases (49.5%), respondents claim that they might be perceived as an employer of choice but only with regards to some areas of their functioning. These areas most frequently refer to particular candidate's specific competences, which can be used when fulfilling tasks on a job position. One out of every three companies claims that there is nothing that distinguishes them from other companies or that candidates do not identify them as an employer and just respond to job offers they have published.

Of the investigated companies, nearly half (45.5%) declare they do not face any difficulties in hiring people (see Table 5.8). Every

*Table 5.7* Perceived employer brand: candidates' point of view

|  | Share in % |
| --- | --- |
| We are perceived as an employer of choice; many people want to work for us | 17.50 |
| We are perceived as an employer of choice but only in some areas | 49.50 |
| Candidates identify us as a potential employer, but there is nothing that distinguishes us from others | 20.00 |
| Candidates do not identify us as an employer; they respond to job offers we publish | 13.00 |

*Table 5.8* Difficulties in recruitment

|  | Share in % |
|---|---|
| No, candidates apply for the job in our companies on their own, without responding to job offers | 0.00 |
| No, there are many candidates responding to our job offers, out of whom we may choose those that best meet our expectations | 13.00 |
| Rather not, every job advertisement published evokes interest in candidates that meet our expectations | 32.50 |
| It depends on the job position, in some cases we have no problems, but in some, it is difficult to find a good candidate | 38.50 |
| Yes, despite the fact that there are candidates applying for the job, they do not meet our expectations | 12.00 |
| Yes, there are only a few candidates that respond to our job advertisements | 4.00 |

job offer evokes interest in candidates having the required competences. By contrast, there is no response for job offers or candidates do not meet requirements in 16% of SMEs. More than one out of every three companies declares that they face some difficulties in hiring people, but it depends on the job position in question.

Positive outcomes in the HR-related perspective were also confirmed by companies that took part in quantitative research (see Box 5.4).

---

**BOX 5.4 HR-RELATED OUTCOMES**

We have reported positive changes in all aspects of our functioning – sales level, activity range, our employees' competences and cooperation. These are a better working climate and good relationships between employees, which are the driving force behind all our positive changes. Paying more attention to who you hire is crucial. Every employee needs to know why they are with us and how their work impacts upon our functioning. (Company J)

We are very innovative in HR-related issues. We have implemented many changes referring to work space organisation, assuring work–life balance, employment flexibility and work scheduling. (Company K)

*(Continued)*

---

> Innovations refer to employees' management. We do not want to follow any strict procedures. It is not our way of thinking that we develop any scheme and then decide 'ok, let's follow it'. We continuously analyse with whom we are working and we try to modify our employment relations and HRM practices to meet employees' expectations. (Company E)

## Approaches to Talent Management

In order to evaluate how a particular scope, structure and configuration of talent management practices impacts upon the performance of SMEs, in-depth analyses were conducted. Through this analysis, six clusters of companies were identified with regard to their approach to talent management. Such categorisation was made on the basis of the following eight indicators:

1   *Strategic importance of talent management* refers to the declared importance of talents by the organisation and to the level of compliance to the given firm's overall strategy.
2   *Source of talent* allows the identification of main talent indicators which may rely on competences (knowledge, skills, attitudes and abilities) or on performance, or both.
3   *Consistency and inclusion* made it possible to distinguish between companies that run talent management activities either systematically or incidentally and whether they apply the inclusive or exclusive approach.
4   *Main activities in talent management* refers to the scope of activities undertaken in talent management. It provides a better understanding of the complexity of talent management practices and gives an answer to the question of whether SMEs treat talent management as a system covering all the main processes (e.g. acquisition, training and development, appraisal, remuneration, motivation, career planning) or only apply particular activities.
5   *Scope of talents' tasks and roles* refers to the scope of talents' duties. It shows how a talented person is perceived in an organisation and if talents fulfil specialised tasks (compliant with their competences); managerial duties (being responsible for coordinating the work of others); any other special duties that may be applicable.

6  *Differentiation of talent-related HR activities* provides information about the extent to which talent management practices are diversified in comparison to HRM practices offered to other employees.
7  *Main areas of development* refer to the main goals of talents' development and future activities as well as the roles that will be dedicated to them.
8  *Talent competences* enable the identification of talents' crucial and important competences – those that are linked with the scope of their roles, tasks and expectations concerning future duties.

On the basis of the above-mentioned criteria, six clusters referring to the approach to talent management were identified. These are as follows: *High-Performance Manager, High-Performance Specialist, High-Potential Internal Consultant, High-Potential Specialist, High-Potential Manager* and *Creator*. An overview of these approaches is presented in Table 5.9 and discussed in detail below.

### 'High-Performance Manager' Cluster (N = 30)

In most of these companies, talent refers to high performers (83%). Almost all companies (93%) claim that talents play a crucial role in achieving expected goals and running a business. All companies in this cluster claim to have linked talent management practices with the overall business strategy. In this cluster, talent management can be both inclusive (in 40% of SMEs) or exclusive (30%) and it is run systematically. Of these companies, 80% have a HRM strategy, but in only 37% of cases does it have a written form. SMEs from this cluster implement talents' tailored training (70%), remuneration (87%), appraisal (80%) and career planning (77%). However, the main activity undertaken in talent management programmes is talent identification (63%) and training (43%). The main goal of development programmes is to enhance managerial competences. Talents' roles and tasks are in general directly related to their qualifications and job requirements (77%). Most companies in this cluster find all listed competences to be crucial.

### 'High-Performance Specialist' Cluster (N = 31)

In this cluster, performance (55%), the ability to fulfil a wide scope of tasks (48%) and a high level of job-related qualifications (42%)

*Table 5.9* Main differences between clusters

| Criteria of clusters' differentiation | Clusters | | | | | |
|---|---|---|---|---|---|---|
| Main talent indicator | Results | Results | Competences | Competences | Competences | Competences |
| Strategic importance of talent management | Definitely yes, talents are perceived as crucial and TM practices are linked with firm's strategy | Rather yes, talents are perceived as important and most firms link talent management practices with firm's strategy | Rather yes, talents are perceived as important and most firms link talent management practices with firm's strategy | Definitely yes, talents are perceived as crucial; however, talent management in general is not linked with firm's strategy | Definitely yes, talents are perceived as crucial and talent management practices are linked with firm's strategy | Rather not, in half of the companies, talent management practices are loosely linked with strategic goals |
| Consistency and inclusion | Systematic and inclusive or exclusive | Systematic and inclusive or exclusive | Sporadically introduced | Systematic and mainly inclusive | Systematic and inclusive | Exclusive and sporadically introduced |
| Differentiation of talent-related HR activities | Yes | No | In general no, only development is tailored | Yes | Yes | No |
| Main activities in talent management | Identification and development | Identification and acquisition | Appraisal and career path planning | Acquisition and identification | All activities | Talent identification |

| Main area of development | Managerial competences | Competences related to task fulfilment | General management and firm functioning | Managerial competences | Managerial competences | Lack of clearly defined aim |
|---|---|---|---|---|---|---|
| Scope of talents' tasks and roles | Mainly referring to qualifications but occasionally also others | Strictly connected with tasks on a given position | Managing or coordination of tasks and processes | Mainly referring to qualifications or coordinating processes | Managing or coordination of tasks and processes | Strictly connected with tasks on a given position |
| Talents' competences | *Crucial:* Subject-specific knowledge, business knowledge, language skills, communication skills, relationship building, cooperation, planning, effectiveness-related competences | *Important:* Subject-specific knowledge, relationship building, cooperation, effectiveness-related competences | *Crucial:* Subject-specific knowledge *Important:* business knowledge, communication skills, relationship building, cooperation, planning, effectiveness-related competences | *Important:* Subject-specific knowledge and planning | *Crucial:* Subject-specific knowledge and planning *Important:* business knowledge, language skills, communication skills, relationship building, effectiveness-related competences, cooperation | *Important:* Subject-specific knowledge, relationship building, cooperation and planning |
| Meaning of talents | High-Performance Manager | High-Performance Specialist | High-Potential Internal Consultant | High-Potential Specialist/Process leader | High-Potential Manager | Creator |

The initial version of this synthesis was published in Pauli and Pocztowski (2019).

are most frequently highlighted as talent indicators. The majority of respondents (84%) declare that a high impact on firms' functioning is attributed to talented employees. The vast majority of companies (90%) have linked talent management with the overall strategy. Companies in this cluster do not introduce a coherent talent management system. Some run systematic talent management programmes for all employees (26%), but others take differentiated, occasional actions (22%). More than half of the companies (58%) have defined key strategic goals for HRM activities in some areas. The strategy is defined in 39% of cases (19% have it in a written form). There are no specific actions referring to remuneration, appraisal, training or career planning introduced for talents. The main activity is talent acquisition and recruitment (71%), as well as identification (45%). Talents are responsible for fulfilling tasks directly related to their qualifications (in 52% of companies in this group). Developmental programmes for talents are aimed at increasing the level of skills required for task fulfilment in 90% of cases. In this cluster, *subject-specific knowledge, relationship building, cooperation* and *effectiveness-related competences* are perceived to be important.

### 'High-Potential Internal Consultant' Cluster (N = 30)

In this cluster, a talent for SMEs can be a person who has above-average skills and abilities (50%), or one who can have a significant impact on others (43%). The majority of respondents (80%) declare that a high impact on firms' functioning is attributed to talented employees. Almost all companies (93%) have linked talent management with the overall strategy. Most frequently (47%), these companies introduce talent management programmes sporadically when a need arises. More than one out of every three companies (77%) have defined key strategic goals for HRM activities in some areas. The strategy is defined in only 20% of cases (7% have it in a written form). Generally, these companies do not differentiate between remuneration, appraisals and career planning for talents; however, most of them (83%) introduce tailored training programmes. The most frequently introduced talent management activities are appraisals (33%) and career planning (33%). Recruitment and training activities are run by 27% of companies. A talented employee is, in most of these companies, responsible for coordinating tasks and specified functions or for managing processes (53%). Development activities focus on enhancing knowledge concerning the company as a whole (67%) and developing managerial competences (40%). In this cluster, *subject-specific knowledge* is regarded as crucial and *business-specific knowledge, language skills, communicational skills, relationship building, cooperation, planning* and *effectiveness-related competences* are perceived to be important.

### 'High-Potential Specialist' Cluster (N = 49)

In this cluster, a talented employee can be a person who has wide knowledge (57%), above-average skills (57%) or have an impact on others (45%). In more than half (57%) of the companies, talents are perceived as having a crucial impact on firms' functioning and in 43%, they are regarded as being important. However, only 46% have linked talent management with the overall strategy. Most companies run systematic talent management activities available for all employees (53%). The vast majority have a HRM strategy (84%), but in only 12% of cases is it written down. The majority of companies have training programmes tailored for talents (59%), remuneration system (82%), appraisals (90%) and career path planning (96%). The main activities included in talent management programmes are recruitment and selection (65%), identification (51%) and training (49%). A talented person is responsible for fulfilling tasks referring to a job position, but they are sometimes asked to take part in some other processes (47%). Training programmes are frequently aimed at enhancing managerial competences (94%). In this cluster, *subject-specific knowledge, relationship building* and *planning* are perceived to be important. The other competences are most frequently evaluated as applicable.

### 'High-Potential Manager' Cluster (N = 38)

In general, these companies perceive a talent as a person of above-average skills (45%) and a highly qualified specialist (47%). In more than two out of every three (68%) companies, talents are perceived as having a crucial impact on firms' functioning. Almost all of the companies (97%) have linked talent management with the overall strategy. Most frequently, these companies run inclusive, planned and complex talent management programmes (47%), or activities that are planned but available only to chosen employees (29%). The majority of SMEs in this cluster (60%) have a HRM strategy, but only 29% are in a written form. Most of these companies (87%) differentiate the remuneration system for talents. They may also introduce different appraisal systems (84%). Companies in this cluster can provide talents with tailored career paths (82%), most of them with tailored training programmes (55%) mostly aimed at developing managerial competences. Talent management consists of talent acquisition (71%), training (61%), remuneration (47%), appraisals (42%) and career planning (42%), which means it is fairly complex. In the majority of these SMEs, a talented employee is responsible for managing processes (53%). Companies in this cluster find *subject-specific knowledge, business-specific knowledge, cooperation* and *planning* crucial. Moreover, *language skills, relationship building* and *effectiveness-related competences* are important.

### *'Creator' Cluster (N = 22)*

In this cluster, a talent is perceived mainly as a creative person able to implement modifications and innovations (46%) or as a high performer (32%). The highest share of companies (41%) that applied this approach do not rather attribute a high importance to talented people. Almost one out of every three (32%) believes that talents may be important and have an impact upon the given firm's functioning. Half of the companies have linked talent management with the overall business strategy. These companies tend to introduce talent management programmes sporadically when a need arises (36%). They are usually focused on talent identification (64%). More than half of the companies (59%) have defined key strategic goals regarding HRM activities in some areas. The strategy is defined in 14% of cases (5% of which have it written down). These companies do not apply specified talent management practices. They do not usually differentiate training programmes (73% have the same programmes for talents and other employees), remuneration (86%), their appraisal system (95%) or career planning (96%). A talent is responsible mostly for fulfilling tasks that directly relate to their qualifications. Companies in this cluster find *subject-specific knowledge, relationship building, cooperation, planning* and *effectiveness-related competences* important; other competences are applicable.

The cluster characteristics presented above prove how differentiated talent management practices in SMEs are. Despite the fact that six clusters have been identified, none of them are coherent enough to describe a common path for all SMEs included within it.

## Talent Management Approaches and Small and Medium Enterprises' Performance

### *Outcomes of SMEs that Applied the 'High-Performance Manager' Approach*

SMEs that applied this approach do not confirm achieving outcomes that may prove their high competitiveness. Regarding organisational outcomes, nearly half of these companies have not introduced any changes referring to products/services or internal processes, and nearly one out of every three companies has not introduced changes in the technology used. Slight modifications referring to internal processes were introduced in 30% of SMEs, modifications referring to products/services in 40% and those referring to technology in 50% of cases. Thus, it can be concluded that the implementation of talent management practices does not significantly contribute to higher achievements from the perspective of organisational outcomes.

Similar conclusions can be drawn on the basis of data referring to business performance outcomes. The vast majority of companies that applied the 'High-Performance Manager' approach declared no changes in the investigated indicators. The share of companies claiming that particular indicators remained stable ranged from 63% to 80%. Thus, such data confirms that from the business perspective, the implementation of talent management practices does not result in higher performance.

The results of the HR-related outcomes analysis are in line with those referring to organisational and business performance. The direct impact of implementing talent management practices on HR-related indicators cannot be traced. Nearly half of the respondents (57%) evaluate employees' engagement as high. SMEs that applied this approach most frequently claim that their employees perceive them as companies that provide developmental opportunities (47%). However, it is very difficult to find any other factors that can build a coherent image. Only 7% of companies in this cluster believe they are perceived as an employer of choice; however, 63% believe they have a very good employer brand in some areas. The same share of companies (63%) claim they do not face any difficulties with hiring, and 30% claim that potential obstacles depend on the job position.

On the basis of the gathered data, it is impossible to indicate a clear interdependence between the implementation of 'High-Performance Manager' approach to talent management and firm performance when taking into account all these three perspectives (organisational, business- and HR-related).

### Outcomes of SMEs that Applied the 'High-Performance Specialist' Approach

In this group of companies, the vast majority have introduced changes in products/services offered, technology and internal processes. As many as 61%, declare they have modified products/ services to some extent and 13% have introduced significant modifications. A similar share of companies have introduced changes in technology (slight changes – 68%, significant changes – 10%). The most significant changes in organisational perspective outcomes were ascribed to internal processes. The vast majority of these companies (81%) have introduced slight changes and only 3% have introduced significant changes.

When taking into account business performance, most of these companies declare that the investigated indicators have remained stable over the previous five years. The share of companies claiming that *sales volume, profit level, overall financial conditions* and *brand recognition* have not changed, ranged from 68% to 74%. An increase in *sales value* was confirmed by 30% of SMEs in this cluster and 39% claimed they have noticed a rise in the *number of customers.*

In these companies, the internal HR-related outcomes are evaluated better than external outcomes. The vast majority (87%) evaluate their employees' engagement as very high and 61% claim that they offer very interesting tasks. However, only 39% perceive themselves generally as employers of choice and 19% assume they have a good employer brand in only some areas. Half of these companies claim they face no difficulties when hiring people and 32% report that it may depend on the job position.

On the basis of these analyses, it can be concluded that companies applying the 'High-Performance Specialist' approach achieve the highest results in the organisational perspective as in this group of indicators, positive changes were most frequently indicated.

### Outcomes of SMEs that Applied the 'High-Potential Internal Consultant' Approach

SMEs included in this cluster confirm positive changes in relation to the organisational perspective. As many as 67% of companies claim that they have introduced slight changes in the products/services they offer and 13% of the companies have introduced significant changes.

Similarly, 70% of the companies have introduced slight and 7% significant changes in the technology they use. The highest level of modifications referred to internal processes. Among companies that have introduced these modifications, 40% declare they have made slight changes and 37% report they have introduced significant changes. However, 3% of respondents confirm they have conducted a complex reorganisation of their internal processes and introduced complex systems to link all processes running in the organisation. This enables increasing the effectiveness of their functioning.

The analysis of business performance also made it possible to identify possible changes. In indicators referring to *number of customers, brand recognition* and *overall financial condition*, the share of companies confirming an increase exceeded 60% (61%, 66% and 67%, respectively). Additionally, in the case of *brand recognition* and *number of customers*, one out of every four companies confirms that it has remained stable (in the case of *overall financial* condition, it was 15%). Thus, it can be concluded that only 10–18% have reported negative trends referring to these three indicators over the previous five years. When analysing profit level, nearly half (48%) declare an increase and 30% declare stability. Interestingly, in this cluster, only 34% of companies have declared an increase in *products/services sales volume* and 41% in *sales value* (stability was reported by 41% and 21%, respectively). This means that in the case of 25–38% of companies, there was a decrease in sales-related indicators, which could be the reason why 31% of companies in this cluster report a decline in the *number of employees*.

Despite the fact that an increase in organisational and business performance can be identified, positive changes in HR-related perspective cannot be easily traced. Only just over half of the investigated companies (57%) have evaluated their employees' engagement as high. SMEs in this cluster most frequently claim that they are perceived by their employees as companies in which there is a *friendly atmosphere* (40%) and which *offer attractive work conditions* (40%). Half of the companies believe they are perceived as an employer of choice in some areas of their functioning, but only 10% claim they are in general employers of choice. This may result in some difficulties in hiring people. Only 27% of these companies claim not to face any problems when acquiring new employees and 50% claim it depends upon job position.

On the basis of the conducted analyses, it can be concluded that in the group of companies that applied the 'High-Potential Internal Consultant' approach, talent management practices impact upon business and organisational performance rather than upon HR-related outcomes.

### Outcomes of SMEs that Applied the 'High-Potential Specialist' Approach

Most of the companies included in this cluster confirm improvements with regard to organisational issues. As many as 63% have introduced changes in products and services (slight changes – 61%, significant changes – 2%), 63% in technology (slight changes – 57%, significant changes – 6%), and 73% in services (55% to some extent, 18% significant ones). Thus, it can be concluded that all the areas of organisational outcomes have developed almost equally.

When taking into account business performance, companies that applied the *High-Potential Specialist* approach confirm positive changes in five out of seven indicators. The best outcomes refer to *sales value* and *profit level*. In the first case, almost two out of every three companies (65%) indicate an increase (18% claimed it remained stable), while in the second, this value was 60% (38% claim it remained stable). Nearly half of the SMEs in this cluster report an increase in the *number of customers* (52%) and *brand recognition* (53%). In both cases, the number of companies reporting that the indicator remained stable is one out of every three SMEs. The *sales volume* and *overall financial condition* were indicators in which the level of firms confirming an increase was the lowest. However, it should be stressed that only 18% of companies sold less than before and 22% of companies found their *overall financial condition* to be worse.

With regard to HR-related outcomes, significant positive changes cannot be traced. Only 53% of companies in this cluster evaluated their employees' engagement as high. Moreover, only 39% claim not to have difficulties with hiring employees, and in 35% of cases, potential problems are related to job positions. However, these companies clearly indicate their employer brand. More than half (57%) declare they are perceived as companies in which there is a friendly climate and 65% offer interesting tasks. Additionally, 71% believe themselves to be an employer of choice in some areas and 10% believe they are the first-choice employer in general.

### Outcomes of SMEs that Applied the 'High-Potential Manager' Approach

In this group of companies, the vast majority have implemented changes in areas relating to organisational performance. The lowest changes can be ascribed to technology as only 42% of companies have introduced slight changes and 21% have introduced significant changes. However, when taking into account products and services, 58% declare they have introduced slight and 16% declare introducing significant changes. Moreover, 37% of companies claim they have introduced slight changes in internal processes; 45% have modified them significantly and 3% have introduced complex systems.

From the business performance perspective, in each of the analysed criteria, the highest share relates to companies claiming they have observed an increase. As many as 59% of companies claimed they observe an upswing in the *profit level*, which may stem from a boost in *sales value* and *volume* (62% and 63%, respectively). Additionally, 67% of companies in this cluster confirm an increase in *brand recognition*, which may cause a rise in the *number of customers* (confirmed by 70% of companies). Positive changes in all these indicators may result in an increase in the *overall financial condition*, which was confirmed by 60% of the respondents.

SMEs that applied the 'High-Potential Manager' approach also evaluated their HR-related outcomes as being high. The employee engagement level was assessed as high in 61% of cases. Moreover, these companies are perceived as employers providing developmental opportunities (53%) or interesting projects in which an employee may be involved (50%). Nearly one out of every three companies (29%) believe themselves to be perceived as an employer of choice, and additionally, 55% claim they are an employer of choice in some areas. This may result in a low level of difficulties in hiring people as 53% declare they do not have any problems and 34% state that some problems may refer to a particular job position.

### Outcomes of SMEs that Applied the 'Creator' Approach

Companies in this cluster introduced changes in organisational outcomes to the lowest extent. Nearly half of them have not implemented any modifications in the products/services offered or in the technology. Some improvements in internal processes were implemented in only 41% of the companies.

Within the companies that have applied the 'Creator' approach, a decrease in most of business indicators was confirmed. As many as 39% claim they have fewer *customers* (in 33%, the number remained stable), 33% declare a decrease in *sales volume* (33% claim it remained stable) and 22% reported lower *sales value* (in 56%, it remained stable). This resulted in negative trends in the *profit level* (41% declare a decrease, 35% declare that it remained stable) and in the *overall financial condition* (33% report a decrease, 44% claim it remained stable). The only indicator that received a relatively positive evaluation is brand recognition – 33% of companies declare an increase and 56% declare it remaining at the same level.

Similarly, when taking into account the HR-related outcomes perspective, negative trends can be more frequently traced. Only 36% of the companies have reported their employees' engagement as high, and nearly one out of every three has assessed it as moderate or low. As many as 64% of SMEs in this cluster are unable to indicate how they are perceived by employees. Similarly, 45% claim that candidates do not identify them as a potential employer and 32% believe that there is nothing that distinguishes them from others. This may result in a situation in which only 27% of companies face no difficulties in hiring new employees.

The summary of outcomes reported by companies clustered into particular approaches to talent management is presented in Table 5.10.

It can be concluded that the companies that applied the 'High-Potential Manager Approach' have reported the best outcomes. These companies have implemented changes in the products/services they offer, in the technology they use and, to the highest extent, in their internal processes. Additionally, these SMEs have reported the achievement of the highest increase in business performance indicators. The share of companies that have reported positive trends in each indicator accounted for 59–70%. Moreover, in these companies, the level of employee engagement was evaluated as being very high; they have reported an increase in employment and they face relatively few difficulties in hiring people. Moreover, they are most frequently perceived as employers of choice.

Companies that are perceived to be less effective are those that implemented the *Creator* approach. Of these companies, the majority claimed to *remain stable* in most of the indicators or they reported a decrease. This refers to all of the investigated perspectives: organisational, business and HR-related.

Regarding the remaining four approaches, some consistency can be observed. Companies that pay more attention to performance in talent management (those that have applied the 'High-Performance Manager' or the 'High-Performance Specialist' approach) claim they obtain satisfactory levels of organisational and HR-related outcomes. By contrast, companies that pay more attention to potential as talent indicator ('High-Potential Internal Consultant' or 'High-Potential Specialist') claim they achieve higher results in business performance indicators. Thus, it can be concluded that the

*Table 5.10* A comparison of outcomes reported by SMEs applying particular approaches to talent management

| Criterion | High-Performance Manager | | High-Performance Specialist | | High-Potential Internal Consultant | | High-Potential Specialist/Process Leader | | High-Potential Manager | | Creator | |
|---|---|---|---|---|---|---|---|---|---|---|---|---|
| **Organisational outcomes** | Slight | Significant | Slight | Significant | Slight | Significant | Slight | Significant | Slight | Significant | Slight | Significant |
| Changes in: | | | | | | | | | | | | |
| Products, services | 40 | 13 | 61 | 13 | 67 | 13 | 61 | 2 | 58 | 16 | 45 | 5 |
| Technology | 50 | 17 | 68 | 10 | 70 | 7 | 57 | 6 | 42 | 21 | 50 | 0 |
| | 30 | 13 | 81 | 3 | 40 | 37 | 55 | 18 | 37 | 45 | 41 | 18 |
| Processes | Complex system – 7 | | Complex system – 3 | | Complex system – 3 | | Complex system – 0 | | Complex system – 3 | | Complex system – 0 | |
| **Business outcomes** | No changes | Increase | No changes | Increase | No changes | Increase | No changes | Increase | No changes | Increase | No changes | Increase |
| Sales volume | 63 | 30 | 74 | 23 | 41 | 34 | 35 | 47 | 20 | 63 | 44 | 22 |
| Sales Value | 67 | 27 | 58 | 29 | 21 | 41 | 18 | 65 | 14 | 62 | 56 | 22 |
| Profit level | 63 | 30 | 71 | 26 | 30 | 48 | 38 | 60 | 28 | 59 | 35 | 24 |
| Number of customers | 70 | 17 | 61 | 39 | 25 | 62 | 35 | 52 | 20 | 70 | 33 | 38 |
| Financial condition | 73 | 20 | 71 | 29 | 15 | 67 | 33 | 45 | 27 | 60 | 44 | 22 |
| Brand recognition | 77 | 17 | 68 | 29 | 24 | 66 | 33 | 53 | 20 | 67 | 56 | 33 |

(Continued)

## HR-related outcomes

| Criterion | High-Performance Manager | High-Performance Specialist | High-Potential Internal Consultant | High-Potential Specialist/Process Leader | High-Potential Manager | Creator |
|---|---|---|---|---|---|---|
| Employees engagement | Moderate 37; High 57 | Moderate 13; High 87 | Moderate 37; High 57 | Moderate 43; High 53 | Moderate 24; High 61 | Moderate 32; High 36 |
| Number of employees | No changes 80; Increase 13 | No changes 71; Increase 36 | No changes 31; Increase 38 | No changes 29; Increase 51 | No changes 33; Increase 57 | No changes 71; Increase 18 |
| Difficulties with recruitment | Depending on position 30; No 63 | Depending on position 32; No 50 | Depending on position 50; No 27 | Depending on position 35; No 39 | Depending on position 34; No 53 | Depending on position 59; No 27 |
| Perceived employer image – by candidates | Employer of choice in some areas 63; Employer of choice 7 | Employer of choice in some areas 19; Employer of choice 39 | Employer of choice in some areas 50; Employer of choice 10 | Employer of choice in some areas 71; Employer of choice 10 | Employer of choice in some areas 55; Employer of choice 29 | Employer of choice in some areas 14; Employer of choice 9 |
| Perceived employer image – by employees – company which: | Creates developmental opportunities – 47 | Offers interesting jobs – 61 | Creates friendly atmosphere – 40; Creates attractive working conditions – 40 | Creates friendly atmosphere – 57; Offers interesting tasks – 65 | Creates developmental opportunities – 53; Involves in varied projects – 50 | We cannot indicate how we are perceived by our employees – 64 |

*Note*: Data in %.

applied approach derives from the firms' market situation. Those companies that have potential in the form of human and organisational capital tend to focus on acquiring and developing talents who may ensure better business performance. Companies that achieve an expected level of business performance try to find talents who may increase the firms' market potential by developing both organisational and human capital.

Applying the 'Creator' approach may stem from a need to find people who can be a driving force for complex firms' reorganisation as these companies report the lowest level of performance in all three perspectives. In such cases, talents may ensure both internal development and higher competitiveness.

Such a conclusion is in line with previous studies concerning HRM practices in SMEs. According to these studies, HRM in SMEs is reactive and based upon emerging needs.

# 6    Closing Remarks

Talent management in SMEs is very diverse when taking into account the way talent is defined, the approaches applied, as well as the scope and complexity of practices introduced. Such a diversity in talent management stems from the specificity of SMEs themselves and from the context these companies operate in. Both these issues are widely discussed in the subject-specific literature. The research conducted on a sample of Polish SMEs confirmed conclusions drawn by other authors investigating talent management in such companies (Festing et al., 2013; Valverde et al., 2013; Krishnan & Scullion, 2017). Some general findings based on the research conducted by the authors are presented in this chapter. They refer to the research questions from the introduction section.

As far as the meaning of talent in investigated companies is concerned, it can be stated that the most frequently reported indicators are above-average skills and abilities combined with occupational experience, and firm- or subject-specific competences together with high effectiveness. Such an understanding of talent proves that in most SMEs, talent is perceived as acquired, situational, feasible to develop and attributed to a person rather than to organisational roles or positions. This means that talent can be developed with the use of specific tools and actions and can be crafted according to a firm's expectations.

Approaches to talent management and practices stemming from these approaches are determined by contextual factors, be they internal or external. Most of the investigated SMEs operate in new, emerging sectors in which intangible resources are of primary importance in assuring competitive advantage. The most frequently mentioned factors that can build competitive advantage are innovativeness and the time-to-react to changes. Within the external context, the most important factors (that imply the shape of talent management) refer to the situation on the labour market and difficulties with acquiring employees for specialist positions. However, the research results confirmed that the investigated companies try to adjust their working conditions and environment to the expectations of employees and candidates. This has a positive impact on their employer brand and supports attracting valuable candidates.

Among factors referring to the internal context, the most impactful are the low level of organisational structure formalisation, the highly centralised decision-making process and the crucial role of the owner or CEO in running the business. Moreover, many of the investigated SMEs focus on executing processes that are the core of their business and outsource other, supportive functions such as *accounting, payroll, human resource management, IT, marketing and promotion*. The conducted analyses confirmed that SMEs operate in various contexts. This supports the conclusions drawn by other authors that contextual factors have an impact upon talent management (Gallardo-Gallardo et al., 2019; Thunnissen et al., 2013; Thunnissen & Gallardo-Gallardo, 2019).

The scope of activities, undertaken within talent management, is very wide and includes actions that are at the core of human resource management in general. It can be concluded that within all the activities addressed to a wide range of employees, some practices tailored to talents are introduced. The selection of these practices stems from both the business needs and the labour market situation. In the group of investigated SMEs, the inclusive as well as exclusive approach was applied. This supports other authors' findings that in SMEs, both approaches are implemented (Festing et al., 2013; Valverde et al., 2013).

It is worth noting that the scope and specificity of talent management practice change when taking into account their tenure. On the basis of the conducted research, it can be concluded that the longer talent management practices exist in a company, the more complex they are. Companies with more mature talent management practices apply a wide range of tools and actions aimed at supporting and executing actions in investigated talent management subprocesses. Additionally, talent management practices are shaped by the specificity of talents' tasks and duties. SMEs in which talents are responsible for executing specialist and managerial tasks or roles more actively introduce talent management practices.

The outcomes of talent management were presented with the use of six clusters (referring to approaches to talent management) and three perspectives (business, organizational and HR-related).

The characteristics of the clusters proved how differentiated are approaches to talent management in SMEs. Despite the fact that six clusters have been identified, none of them are coherent enough to describe a common path for all SMEs included within it. The gathered data confirms that in general, the investigated companies report business outcomes at more than a satisfactory level. It can be concluded that the vast majority of the investigated companies confirmed the existence of positive trends in indicators with regard to organisational outcomes. The evaluation of HR-related outcomes with the use of such indicators as *turnover, employee engagement* and *employer brand* showed that there are significant differences between particular clusters. Notwithstanding this, the highest share of companies claimed that there have not been any changes in the employment level within the previous five years. However, one out of every three companies declared a rise in the number of employees. More than half of the examined SMEs evaluate their employees' engagement in fulfilling tasks as high or very high. The most frequently mentioned features of SMEs are friendly climate, the possibility to fulfil interesting tasks, developmental opportunities and the possibility to be involved in the execution of diverse projects. Thus, the employer brand of investigated SMEs is built mainly on the basis of the diverse and wide range of tasks offered to employees, developmental opportunities and informal, customised working conditions.

Theoretical considerations and the analysis of research results presented in this book add value to the debate on talent management in SMEs. They also prove that the research on talent management in such companies should be continued. The presented findings and conclusions may inspire scientists to raise new research questions and develop hypotheses. One of the issues that should be addressed and investigated in more detail is whether talent management practices are mostly determined by common features of SMEs or by national contexts and the specificity of the national markets of particular countries.

The authors are aware of the limitations of the conducted research, but they believe that the provided data, analyses and conclusions will inspire other researchers to develop new perspectives in investigating talent management in SMEs.

# References

Amabile, T. (1997). Motivating creativity in organizations: On doing what you love and loving what you do. *California Management Review, 40*(I), 39–58.

Barney, J. B. (1991). Firm resources and sustained competitive advantage. *Journal of Management, 17*(1), 99–120. DOI: 10.1177/014920639101700108

Bethke-Langenegger, P., Mahler, P. & Staffelbach, B. (2011). Effectiveness of talent management strategies. *European Journal International Management, 5*(5), 524–539. DOI: 10.1504/EJIM.2011.042177

Björkman, I., Ehrnrooth, M., Mäkelä, K., Smale, A. & Sumelius, J. (2013). Talent or not? Employee reactions to talent identification. *Human Resource Management, 52*(2), 195–214. DOI: 10.1002/hrm.21525

Björkman, I. & Mäkelä, K. (2013). Are you willing to do what it takes to become a senior global leader? Explaining willingness to undertake challenging leadership development activities. *European Journal of International Management, 7*(5), 570–586. DOI: 10.1504/EJIM.2013.056478

Bolander, P., Werr, A. & Asplund, K. (2017). The practice of talent management: A framework and typology. *Personnel Review, 46*(8), 1523–1551. DOI: 10.1108/PR-02-2016-0037

Borkowska, S. (Ed.). (2005). *Zarządzanie talentami*. Warszawa, Poland: IPiSS.

Boudreau, J. W. & Ramstad, P. M. (2005). Talentship, talent segmentation, and sustainability: A new HR decision science paradigm for a new strategy definition. *Human Resource Management, 44*(2), 129–136. DOI: 10.1002/hrm.2005

Bowman, C. & Hird, M. (2014). Redefining the boundaries of strategic talent management. In P. Sparrow, H. Scullion & I. Tarique (Eds.), *Strategic talent management: Contemporary issues in international context* (pp. 73–86), Cambridge, UK: Cambridge University Press.

Bratton, A., Garavan, T., D'Annunzio-Green, N. & Grant, K. (2017). IHRD and global talent development. In T. Garavan, A. McCarthy & R. Carbery (Eds.), *Handbook of international human resource development. Context, processes and people* (pp. 417–445), Cheltenham, UK: Elgar.

Calo, T. J. (2008). Talent management in the era of the aging workforce: The critical role of knowledge transfer. *Public Personnel Management, 37*(4), 403–416. DOI: 10.1177/009102600803700403.

Chambers, E. G., Fouldon, M. F., Handfield-Jones, H., Hankins, S. & Michaels III, E. (1998). The war for talent. *The McKinsey Quarterly, 3*, 44–57.

Cheese, P., Thomas, R. T. & Craig, E. (2008). *The talent powered organization: Strategies for globalization, talent management and high performance*. London: Kogan Page.

CIPD (Chartered Institute of Personnel and Development). (2015). *Learning and talent development. Annual survey report*. London: CIPD. Retrieved from https://www.cipd.co.uk/Images/learning-development_2015_tcm18-11298.pdf (accessed 30 January 2020).

Collings, D. G. (2014). Toward mature talent management: Beyond shareholder value. *Human Resource Development Quarterly, 25*(3), 301–319. DOI: 10.1002/hrdq.21198

Collings, D. G. McDonnell, A. & McMackin, J. (2017). Talent management. In P. Sparrow & Sir C. L. Cooper (Eds.), *A Research agenda for human resource management* (pp. 39–54), Cheltenham, UK: Edward Elgar Publishing.

Collings, D. G. & Mellahi, K. (2009). Strategic talent management: A review and research agenda. *Human Resource Management Review, 19*(4), 304–313. DOI: 10.1016/j.hrmr.2009.04.001

Coulson-Thomas, C. (2012). Talent management and building high performance organization. *Industrial and Commercial Training, 44*(7), 429–438. DOI: 10.1108/00197851211268027

Crain, D. W. (2009). Only the right people are strategic asset of the firm. *Strategy and Leadership, 37*(6), 33–38. DOI: 10.1108/10878570911001471

Devins, D. & Gold, J. (2014). Re-conceptualising talent management and development within the context of low paid. *Human Resource Development International, 17*(5), 514–528. DOI: 10.1080/13678868.2014.954191

Dries, N. (2013). The psychology of talent management; A review and research agenda. *Human Resource Management Review, 23*(4), 272–285. DOI: 10.1016/j.hrmr.2013.05.001

Dundon, T. & Wilkinson, A. (2009). Human resource management in small and medium sized enterprises. In D. G. Collings & G. Woods (Eds.), *Human resource management: A critical introduction* (pp. 130–148), London: Rutledge.

Dyer, L. & Reeves, T. (1995). Human resource strategies and firm performance: What do we know and where do we need to go? *The International Journal of Human Resource Management, 6*(3), 656–670. DOI: 10.1080/09585199500000041

Eisenhardt, K. M. & Martin, J. A. (2000). Dynamic capabilities: What are they? *Strategic Management Journal, 21*(10–11), 1105–1121. DOI: 10.1002/1097–0266(200010/11)21:10/11<1105::AID-SMJ133>3.0.CO;2-E

European Commission. (2000). Retrieved from https://ec.europa.eu/growth/content/european-charter-small-enterprises-0_en (accessed 30 January 2020).

European Commission. (2017). Annual Report on European SMEs 2016/2017, DOI: 10.2873/742338

Eurostat. (2020). Active enterprises in the business economy. Retrieved from https://ec.europa.eu/eurostat/statisticsexplained/index.php/Business_demography_statistics#Active_enterprises_in_the_business_economy (accessed 30 January 2020).

Farndale, E., Scullion, H. & Sparrow, P. R. (2010). The role of the corporate HR function in global talent management. *Journal of World Business, 45*(2), 161–168. DOI: 10.1016/j.jwb.2009.09.012

Festing, M., Harsch, K., Schaefer, L. & Scullion, H. (2017). Talent management in small- and medium-sized enterprises. In D. G. Collings, K. Mellahi & W. F. Cascio (Eds.), *The Oxford handbook of talent management* (pp. 478–493), Oxford, UK: Oxford University Press.

Festing, M., Schaefer, L. & Scullion, H. (2013). Talent management in medium-sized German companies: An explorative study and agenda for future research, *The International Journal of Human Resource Management, 24*(9), 1872–1893. DOI: 10.1080/09585192.2013.777538

Gagné, F. (2000). Understanding the complex choreography of talent development through DGMT–based analysis. In K. A. Heller (Ed.), *International handbook of giftedness and talent* (2nd ed., pp. 67–80), Oxford, UK: Elsevier.

Gagné, F. (2004). Transforming gifts into talent: The DMGT as a developmental theory. *High Ability Studies, 15*(2), 119–147. DOI: 10.1080/135981 3042000314682

Galbreath, J. (2005). Which resources matter the most to firm success? An exploratory study of resource-based theory. *Technovation, 25*(9), 979–987. DOI: 10.1016/j.technovation.2004.02.008

Gallardo-Gallardo, E., Dries, N. & Gonzalez-Cruz, T. (2013). What is the meaning of 'talent' in the world of work. *Human Resource Management Review, 23*(4), 290–300. DOI: 10.1016/j.hrmr.2013.05.00

Gallardo-Gallardo, E., Thunnissen, M. & Scullion, H. (2019, July). Talent management: Context matters. *The International Journal of Human Resource Management.* DOI: 10.1080/09585192.2019.1642645

Glaister, A. J., Karacay, G., Demirbag, M. & Tatoglu, E. (2018). HRM and performance: The role of talent management as a transmission mechanism in an emerging market context. *Human Resource Management Journal, 28*(1), 148–166. DOI: 10.1111/1748–8583.12170

Gonzalez-Cruz, T., Martinez-Fuentes, C. & Pardo-del-Val, M. (2009). La gestión del talent en la empresa industrial Española. *Economia Industrial, 374,* 21–35.

Heneman, R. L, Tansky, J. W. & Camp, M. (2000). Human resource management practices in small and medium-sized enterprises: Unanswered questions and future research perspectives. *Entrepreneurship Theory and Practice, 25*(1), 11–26. DOI: 10.1177/104225870002500103

Hinrichs, J. R. (1966). *High-talent personnel: Managing a critical resource.* Vermont, VT: American Management Association.

Huselid, M., Beatty, R. & Becker, B. (2005). A players or a positions? The strategic logic of workforce management. *Harvard Business Review, 83*(12), 110–117.

Huselid, M. A. & Becker, B. E. (2011). Bridging micro and macro domains: Workforce differentiation and strategic human resource management. *Journal of Management, 37*(2), 421–428. DOI: 10.1177/0149206310373400

Iles, P. (2012). Leadership development and talent management. Fashion statement or fruitful direction. In M. Lee (Ed.), *Human resource development as we know it* (pp. 50–66), New York: Routledge.

Iles, P., Chuai, X. & Preece, D. (2010). Talent management and HRM in multinational companies in Beijing: Definitions, differences and drivers. *Journal of World Business. Special Issue: Global Talent Management, 45*(2), 179–189. DOI: 10.1016/j.jwb.2009.09.014

Ingram, T. (Ed.). (2011). *Zarządzanie talentami. Teoria dla praktyki zarządzania zasobami ludzkimi.* Warszawa, Poland: PWE.

Jamka, B. (2011). *Czynnik ludzki we współczesnym przedsiębiorstwie: zasób czy kapitał? Od zarządzania kompetencjami do zarządzania różnorodnością.* Warszawa, Poland: Oficyna a Wolters Kluwer business.

Jericó, P. (2001). La gestión del talent: Enfoque conceptual y empirico. *Boletin de Estudios Económicos, LVI*(174), 423–441.

Jiang, K., Lepak, D. P., Hu, J. & Baer, J. C. (2012). How does human resource management influence organizational outcomes? A meta-analytic investigation of mediating mechanisms. *The Academy of Management Journal, 55*(6), 1264–1294. DOI: 10.5465/amj.2011.0088

Khoreva, V., Vaiman, V. & Van Zalk, M. (2017). Talent management practice effectiveness: Investigating employee perspective. *Employee Relations, 39*(1), 19–33. DOI: 10.1108/ER-01-2016-0005

Khoreva, V. & Wechtler, H. (2018). HR practices and employee performance: The mediating role of well-being. *Employee Relations, 40*(2), 227–243. DOI: 10.1108/ER-08-2017-0191

Kopeć, J. (2012). *Zarządzanie talentami w przedsiębiorstwie.* Kraków, Poland: Wydawnictwo UEK.

Krishnan, T. N. & Scullion, H. (2017). Talent management and dynamic view of talent in small and medium enterprises. *Human Resource Management Review, 27*(3), 431–441. DOI: 10.1016/j.hrmr.2016.10.003

Lanvin, B. & Monteiro, F. (2019). *The global talent competitiveness index: Entrepreneurial talent and global competitiveness*, INSEAD, The Addecco Group and Tata Communications. Retrieved from https://www.insead.edu/sites/default/files/assets/dept/globalindices/docs/GTCI-2019-Report.pdf (accessed 30 January 2020).

Leczykiewicz, T. (2014). *Zarządzanie talentami w polskich przedsiębiorstwach - wyniki badań.* Raport z badań realizowanych w Wyższej Szkole Bankowej w Poznaniu. Poznań, Poland: WSB w Poznaniu.

Lepak, D. P. & Snell, S. A. (1999). The Human resource architecture: Toward a theory of human capital allocation and development. *Academy of Management Review, 24*(1), 31–48. DOI: 10.2307/259035

Lepak, D. P. & Snell, S. A. (2002). Examining the human resource architecture: The relationships among human capital, employment, and human resource configurations. *Journal of Management, 28*(4), 517–543. DOI: 10.1177/014920630202800403

Lewis, R. E. & Heckman, R. J. (2006). Talent management: A critical review. *Human Resource Management Review, 16*(2), 139–154. DOI: 10.1016/j.hrmr.2006.03.001

Listwan, T. (2005). Zarządzanie talentami - wyzwania dla współczesnych przedsiębiorstw. In S. Borkowska (Ed.), *Zarządzanie talentami* (pp. 19–27), Warszawa, Poland: IPiSS.

Martin, J. & Schmidt, C. (2009). How to keep your top talent. *Harvard Business Review, 8*(5), 54–61.

McDonnell, A., Collings, D. G., Mellahi, K. & Schuler, R. (2017). Talent management: A systematic review and future prospects. *European Journal International Management, 11*(1), 86–128. DOI: 10.1504/EJIM.2017.10001680

Meyers, M. C., van Woerkom, M. & Dries, N. (2013). Talent – Innate or acquired? Theoretical considerations and their implications for talent management. *Human Resource Management Review, 23*(4), 305–321. DOI: 10.1016/j.hrmr.2013.05.003

Miś, A. & Pocztowski, A. (2016). Istota talentu i zarządzania talentami. In A. Pocztowski (Ed.), *Zarządzanie talentami w organizacji* (pp. 38–67), Warszawa, Poland: Wolters Kluwer.

Nijs, S., Gallardo-Gallardo, E., Dries, N. & Sels, L. (2014). A multidisciplinary review into the definition, operalization, and measurement of talent. *Journal of World Business, 49*(2), 180–191. DOI: 10.1016/j.jwb.2013.11.002

Nilsson, S. & Ellström, P. E. (2012). Employability and talent management: Challenges for HRD practices. *European Journal of Training and Development, 36*(1), 26–45. DOI: 10.1108/03090591211192610

Nogalski, B. & Tyburcy, R. (2019). Rozwój koncepcji zarządzania talentami – teoria i praktyka. In A. Wojtczuk-Turek (Ed.), *Zarządzanie kapitałem ludzkim – wyzwania i trendy* (pp. 107–132), Warszawa, Poland: Oficyna Wydawnicza SGH.

Oettingen, G., Marquardt, M. K. & Gollwitzer, P. M. (2012). Mental contrasting turns feedback on creative potential into successful performance. *Journal of Experimental Social Psychology, 48*(5), 990–996. DOI: 10.1016/j.jesp.2012.03.008

Oslo Manual. (2005). Retrieved from http://www.oecd.org/science/inno/2367614.pdf (accessed 30 January 2020).

Patel, P. C. & Cardon, M. S. (2010). Adopting HRM practices and their effectiveness in small firms facing product–market competition. *Human Resource Management, 49*(2), 265–290. DOI: 10.1002/hrm.20346

Pauli, U. (2018). Talent management practices in Polish small and medium enterprises. *Zarządzanie Zasobami Ludzkimi, 6*(125), 97–108.

Pauli, U. (2020). Procesy zarządzania talentami – utrzymywanie i zwalnianie talentów. In A. Miś (Ed.), *Zarządzanie talentami w polskich organizacjach. Architektura systemu* (pp. 104–121), Warszawa, Poland: Wolters Kluwer Polska (in press).

Pauli, U. & Pocztowski, A. (2019). Talent management in SMEs: Exploratory study of polish companies. *Entrepreneurial Business and Economics Review, 7*(4), 199–218. DOI: 10.15678/EBER.2019.070412

Peppermans, R., Vloeberghs, D. & Perkisas, B. (2003). High potential identification policies: An empirical study among Belgian companies. *The Journal of Management Development, 22*(8), 660–678. DOI: 10.1108/02621710310487846

Pike, S., Roos, G. & Marr, B. (2005). Strategic management of intangible assets and value drivers in R&D organizations. *R And D Management, 35*(2), 111–124. DOI: 10.1111/j.1467–9310.2005.00377.x

Pocztowski, A. (2018). *Zarządzanie zasobami ludzkimi. Koncepcje, praktyki, wyzwania.* Warszawa, Poland: PWE.

Pocztowski, A. (Ed.). (2008). *Zarządzanie talentami w organizacji.* Kraków, Poland: Oficyna a Wolters Kluwer Business.

Pocztowski, A. (Ed.). (2016). *Zarządzanie talentami w organizacji* (2nd ed.). Warszawa, Poland: Oficyna a Wolters Kluwer business.

Pocztowski, A. & Buchelt, B. (2009). Talent management in companies functioning in the Polish market. In W. Scroggins, C. Gomez, P. G. Benson, R. L. Oliver & M. J. Turner (Eds.), *Celebrate the tapestry: Diversity in the modern global organization. Proceedings of the 10th International Human Resource Conference* (pp. 1–15). Santa Fe: NMSU Business College.

Pocztowski, A., Miś, A. & Pauli, U. (2019). Zarządzanie talentami w małych i średnich przedsiębiorstwach – praktyki polskich, niemieckich i hiszpańskich firm. In A. Wojtczuk-Turek (Ed.), *Zarządzanie kapitałem ludzkim – wyzwania i trendy* (pp. 133–151), Warszawa, Poland: Oficyna Wydawnicza SGH.

Pocztowski, A. & Pauli, U. (2013). Profesjonalizacja zarządzania zasobami ludzkimi w małych i średnich firmach. *Zarządzanie Zasobami Ludzkimi, 3–4*(92–93), 9–22.

Przytuła, S. (2014). Talent management in Poland: Challenges, strategies and opportunities. In A. Al Ariss (Ed.), *Global talent management. Management for professionals* (pp. 217–235), Cham, Switzerland: Springer.

Purgał-Popiela, J. (2018). Global talent management: Current state of research and trends. *Zarządzanie Zasobami Ludzkimi, 6*(125), 13–28.

Rauch, A. & Hatak, I. (2016). A meta-analysis of different HR-enhancing practices and performance of small and medium sized firms. *Journal of Business Venturing, 31*(5), 485–504. DOI: 10.1016/j.jbusvent.2016.05.005

Roca-Puig, V., Bou-Llusar, J-C., Beltran-Martin, I. & Garcia-Juan, B. (2019). The virtuous circle of human resource investments: A precrisis and postcrisis analysis. *Human Resource Management Journal, 29*(2), 181–198. DOI: 10.1111/1748–8583.12213

Schultz, T. (1961). Investment in human capital. *The American Economic Review, 51*(1), 1–17.

Scullion, H. & Collings, D. G. (2011). *Global talent management.* London, UK: Routledge.

Scullion, H., Collings, D. G. & Caligiuri, P. (2010). Global talent management. *Journal of World Business, 45*(2), 105–108. DOI: 10.1016/j.jwb.2009.09.011

Sheehan, M. (2012). Developing managerial talent. Exploring the link between management talent perceived performance in multinational corporations (MNCs). *European Journal of Training and Development, 36*(1), 66–85. DOI: 10.1108/03090591211192638

Sheehan, M. (2014). Human resource management and performance: Evidence from small and medium-sized firms. *International Small Business Journal, 32*(5), 545–570. DOI: 10.1177/0266242612465454

Shin, D. & Konrad, A. M. (2017). Causality between high-performance work systems and organizational performance. *Journal of Management, 43*(4), 973–997. DOI: 10.1177/0149206314544746

Silzer, R. & Church, A. H. (2009). The pearls and perils of identifying potential. *Industrial and Organizational Psychology, 2*(4), 377–412. DOI: 10.1111/j.1754–9434.2009.01163.x

Silzer, R. & Dowell, B. E. (2010). *Strategy-driven talent management: A leadership imperative.* San Francisco, CA: John Wiley.

Simonton, D. K. (1999). Talent and its development: An emergenic and epigenetic model. *Psychological Review, 106*(3), 435–457. DOI: 10.1037/0033–295X.106.3.435

Skuza, A. (2018). *Zarządzanie talentami a orientacja na uczenie się przedsiębiorstw.* Poznań, Poland: Wydawnictwo UEP.

Skuza, A., Scullion, H. & McDonnell, A. (2013). An analysis of the talent management challenges in a post-communist country: The case of Poland. *The International Journal of Human Resource Management, 24*(3), 453–470. DOI: 10.1080/09585192.2012.694111

Sparrow, P., Scullion, H. & Tarique, I. (2014). Strategic talent management: Future directions. In P. Sparrow, H. Scullion & I. Tarique (Eds.), *Strategic talent management: Contemporary issues in international context* (pp. 278–302), Cambridge, UK: Cambridge University Press.

Sparrow, P. R. & Makram, H. (2015). What is the value of talent management? Building value-driven processes within a talent management architecture. *Human Resource Management Review, 25*(3), 249–263. DOI: 10.1037/0033–295X.106.3.435

Stahl, B., Farndale, E., Morris, S., Paauwe, J., Stiles, P., Trevor, J. & Wright, P. (2012). Six global practices for effective talent management. *MiT Sloan Management Review, 53*(2), 25–42.

Stewart, J. (2017). Developing employees and managers. In G. Rees & P. E. Smith (Eds.), *Strategic human resource management* (2nd ed., pp. 346–380), London: Sage.

Storey, D. J., Saridakis, G., Sen-Gupta, S., Edwards, P. K. & Blackburn, R. A. (2010). Linking HR formality with employee job quality: The role of firm and workplace size. *Human Resource Management, 49*(2), 305–329. DOI: 10.1002/hrm.20347

Strelau, J. (2015). *Różnice indywidualne*. Warszawa, Poland: Wydawnictwo Naukowe Scholar.

Tabor, J. A. (2013). *Zarządzanie talentami w przedsiębiorstwie*. Warszawa, Poland: Poltext.

Tansley, C., Turner, P., Foster, C., Harris, L., Sempik, A., Stewart, J. & Williams, H. (2007). *Talent: Strategy, management, measurement*. London: CIPD.

Tarique, I. & Schuler, R. S. (2010). Global talent management: Literature review, integrative framework, and suggestions for further research. *Journal of World Business, 45*(2), 122–133. DOI: 10.1016/j.jwb.2009.09.019

Thunnissen, M., Boselie, P. & Fruytier, B. (2013). Talent management and the relevance of context: Towards a pluralistic approach. *Human Resource Management Review, 23*(4), 326–336. DOI: 10.1016/j.hrmr.2013.05.004

Thunnissen, M. & Gallardo-Gallardo, E. (2017). *Talent management in practice. An integrated and dynamic approach*. Bingley, UK: Emerald Publishing.

Thunnissen, M. & Gallardo-Gallardo, E. (2019). Rigor and relevance in empirical TM research: Key issues and challenges. *Business Research Quarterly, 22*(3), 171–180. DOI: 10.1016/j.brq.2019.04.003

Thunnissen, M. & Van Arensbergen, P. (2015). A multi-dimensional approach to talent. An empirical analysis of the definition of talent in Dutch academia. *Personnel Review, 44*(2), 182–199. DOI: 10.1108/PR-10–2013–0190

Tyburcy, R. (2015). Dojrzałość procesu zarządzania talentami w organizacjach międzynarodowych. In Cz. Szmidt (Ed.), *Współczesne problemy zarządzania i ekonomii* (pp. 165–180), Warszawa, Poland: Poltext.

Ulrich, D. (2011). Integrated talent management. In K. Oakes & P. Galagan (Eds.), *The executive guide to integrated talent management* (pp. 189–212), Aleksandria, VA: ASTD Press.

Vaiman, V. & Holden, N. J. (2011). Talent management's perplexing landscape in Central and Eastern Europe. In H. Scullion & D. G. Collings (Eds.), *Global talent management* (pp. 178–193), London, UK: Routledge.

Vaiman, V., Scullion, H. & Collings, D. G. (2012). Talent management decision making. *Management Decision, 50*(5), 951–952. DOI: 10.1108/00251741211227663

Vaiman, V., Sparrow, P., Schuler, R. & Collings, D. G. (Eds.). (2018). *Macro talent management: A global perspective on managing talent in developed markets*. New York: Routledge.

Valverde, M., Scullion, H. & Ryan, C. (2013). Talent management in Spanish medium sized organizations. *International Journal of Human Resource Management, 24*(9), 1832–1852. DOI: 10.1080/09585192.2013.777545

Van Ark, B., Mitchel, C. & Ray, R. L. (2016). *CEO challenge 2016: Building capability – Seeking alignment, agility and talent to innovate and grow- CEO strategic implications*. New York, NY: The Conference Board.

Van der Heijde, C. M. & Van der Heiden, B. I. J. M. (2006). A competence-based and multidimensional operationalization and measurement of employability. *Human Resource Management, 45*(3), 449–476. DOI: 10.1002/hrm.20119

Wiblen, S. & McDonnell, A. (2019). Connecting 'talent' meanings and multi-level context: A discursive approach. *The International Journal of Human Resource Management.* Published online: 02 Jul 2019. DOI: 10.1080/09585192.2019.1629988

Williams, M. (2000). *The war for talent: Getting the best from the best.* London, UK: CIPD.

Wood, A. M., Linley, P., Maltby, J., Kashdan, T. B. & Hurling, R. (2011). Using personal and psychological strengths leads to increases in well-being over time: A longitudinal study and the development of the strengths use questionnaire. *Personality and Individual Differences, 50*(1), 15–19. DOI: 10.1016/j.paid.2010.08.004

# Appendix 1
# Sample Characteristics

| Employment | |
|---|---|
| Up to 50 employees | 67.0 |
| 51–100 employees | 26.0 |
| 101–250 employees | 7.0 |

| Sector | |
|---|---|
| Industry | 22.0 |
| Transport | 19.0 |
| Trade | 17.5 |
| Construction | 16.5 |
| Other | 25.0 |

| Activity range | |
|---|---|
| Local | 16.0 |
| Regional | 36.0 |
| National | 35.0 |
| International | 13.0 |

| Company age | |
|---|---|
| 0–3 years | 0.0 |
| 3–5 years | 10.5 |
| 5–8 years | 17.5 |
| 8–12 years | 18.0 |
| 12–16 years | 25.5 |
| Above 16 years | 28.5 |

Data in % of the sample.

# Appendix 2

# Respondents' Profile (Qualitative Study)

| Code | Employment | Respondent | Profile | Sector |
|------|-----------|-----------|---------|--------|
| Company A | 50 | Managing director | Services | HR consulting and advisory |
| Company B | 30 | CEO | Services | Welfare and health |
| Company C | 70 | CEO | Services and trade | Construction |
| Company D | 154 | Marketing specialist | Production | Furniture |
| Company E | 38 | HR executive | Services | Marketing and advertisement |
| Company F | 40 | Senior HR specialist | Services and production | IT |
| Company G | 20 | CEO | Production | IT |
| Company H | 200 | HR business partner | Production and trade | Automotive |
| Company I | 240 | Chief nurse | Services | Medical |
| Company J | 40 | Managing director | Services | IT and marketing |
| Company K | 25 | CEO | Services | Education and research |
| Company L | 54 | Managing director | Production | Printing |
| Company M | 64 | HR specialist | Services | IT |
| Company N | 30 | Managing director | Services | Education |
| Company O | 200 | HR specialist | Production and trade | Automotive |
| Company P | 38 | HR manager | Production services | IT medical |
| Company Q | 250 | CEO and internal consultant | Trade | Pharmaceutical |
| Company R | 40 | HR manager | Services | Cartography |

# Index

Note: **Bold** page numbers refer to tables; *italic* page numbers refer to figures and page numbers followed by "n" denote endnotes.

Printed in the United States
by Baker & Taylor Publisher Services